CAREER INFORMATION AND GUIDANCE AND COUNSELLING

CAREER INFORMATION AND GUIDANCE AND COUNSELLING

Editor

Ramesh Chandra

ISHA BOOKS

DELHI-110 033

Career Information and Guidance and Counselling

ISBN: 81-8205-142-8

Reprinted in 2011 in India by
Isha Books
B-63, Ist Floor
New Gupta Colony
Near DDA Market
Delhi-110009

Printed at: G. Print Process, Delhi

Contents

Preface

Career information, guidance and counselling refers to services that assist individuals, of any age and at any point throughout their lives, to make educational, training and occupational choices and to manage their careers. It includes services provided to those who have not yet entered the labour force, services to job seekers, and services to those who are employed.

Career information and guidance services have traditionally been seen as a public service available from educational institutions, government departments and their agencies. Increasingly, in countries competing in the global economy, common notions about career information and career development are emerging.

Well-organised career information, guidance and counselling services are important both to education systems and to the labour market, as well as to their interface. Within the labour market, well-organised career information, guidance and counselling can: improve the accuracy and accessibility of the information available to individuals about short- and long-term job opportunities. In turn this can improve individual decision making about jobs and about job training opportunities, and improve the allocation of human talents within the labour market.

The present volume embodies latest research and development in the field of career counselling. It will prove useful and informative for academics, educationists, counsellors, teachers and students.

Editor

1

Career Information Counselling

Career information, guidance and counselling refers to services that assist individuals, of any age and at any point throughout their lives, to make educational, training and occupational choices and to manage their careers. It includes services provided to those who have not yet entered the labour force, services to job seekers, and services to those who are employed. It includes a wide range of activities. For example:

— Activities within schools to help students clarify career goals, understand the world of work and develop career-management skills;

— Personal advice, guidance or counselling to assist with decisions about initial courses of study, courses of vocational training, further education and training, initial job choice, job change, or work-force re-entry;

— The organised and systematic use of community members such as employers, alumni, parents and peers to provide occupational and educational advice and information; and

— Print-based, computer-based or on-line services to produce and disseminate information about jobs and careers, courses of study and vocational training to help individuals make career choices.

Career information and guidance services have traditionally been seen as a public service available from educational institutions, government departments and their agencies. Increasingly, in countries competing in the global economy, common notions about career information and career development are emerging:

— It is an individual responsibility - services should help people help themselves manage their career development. This is career self-management;

— It is an ongoing (lifelong) learning process - it is everybody's business and not just something undertaken at a time of crisis;

— It requires worker and learner flexibility and adaptability - changes in the nature of work and employment require that most individuals be prepared to successfully manage several work and learning transitions; and,

— It requires different kinds of tools and services at different points across the life span.

In most countries, there are gaps and overlaps in the career information and guidance services. Availability is uneven. Few countries, it seems, have coherent policies, systems and delivery structures for career information and guidance that support transitions across the span of life, learning and work. Several challenges tend to be common across countries and provide an important context for considering local level services.

— Services to youth and adults have tended to be separate, thereby not reinforcing lifelong access to learning, skill and career development;

— Guidance and career development is both a specialized field and, at the same time, is part of many social services whose focus is not exclusively guidance. Social work, community development and rehabilitation are some examples. The issues of qualifications and assuring quality service are therefore complex;

— Access to ongoing learning opportunities tends to be offered by employers who already have highly skilled workforces. This learning/skill divide has significant economic and social implications;

— There has been an explosion of technology, resulting in more resources devoted to developing career information systems and self-service delivery systems and at least the perception of fewer resources devoted to career counselling and guidance services than ever before;

— In many countries services for youth within the educational systems have often focused on atrisk and marginalized youth and/or on post-secondary bound youth. The school to work bound population has received less emphasis and there is risk they may fall through service cracks once outside the education system itself; and,

— In general, services to adults have been spotty. This is perhaps based on an employment model which is increasingly being questioned, in which adults, once attached to the labour force, were expected to remain attached with permanent and sustainable work and limited career change.

Strategies that focus on a consolidation of services under one national government department or another may not necessarily result in the provision of coherent and seamless career information and guidance services across the life span. Many different kinds of support are likely needed from a variety of agencies. Support is needed where people learn, live and work. And it has to be relevant to their community context.

The Organization for Economic Cooperation and Development (OECD) recognizes that career information and guidance delivery strategies centered at the local (community) level are essential. There are many fine examples of local level cooperation and partnerships that respond to one or more of the challenges outlined earlier.

Well-organised career information, guidance and counselling services are important both to education systems and to the labour market, as well as to their interface. Many arguments in support of this assertion are long-standing, but have been strengthened or refined by more recent developments within education systems and labour markets: both by trends in the ways that these are organised and operate; and by thinking within public-policy and other fora on how they might be organised and operate more effectively.

There are analogies between the importance that well-organised systems of information and advice play in improving the efficiency of education systems and labour markets, and the role that they play in improving the efficiency of financial or other markets. Ignorance is rarely bliss, and information about complex systems is often insufficient by itself. It needs careful organisation and can need sympathetic interpretation if it is to be of value in improving decision making. Context and relevance, trust and shared understanding, each help to mediate information flows and information use.

Within education systems, career education has an important role to play within compulsory education in laying the foundations for lifelong career development. These include knowledge and competences regarding self awareness, the world of work, and making decisions and transitions. Well-organised career information, guidance and counselling are particularly important in postcompulsory education. Here, wider curriculum choice results in more diverse and complex routes into later stages of education, into employment, or into both. Where choices are more complex and their consequences are more costly, effective advice and guidance on educational options, and on links between these options and later occupational destinations, can help to better match individuals' learning choices to their interests, talents and intended destinations. This can help to:

- Reduce dropouts from and back-tracking within education systems, and thus improve internal flows;
- Improve flows between different levels of education, thus raising national levels of educational attainment; and - Improve transitions from education to the labour market.
- These outcomes help to make better use of educational resources, and to increase both individual and social returns to investments in education.

Arguments within education systems for the importance of well-organised systems of career information, guidance and counselling receive greater prominence when national governments commit themselves to implementing policy frameworks that can make lifelong learning for all a reality. This isbecause the notion of lifelong learning stresses:

—The central role of individual learner demands in driving the learning that is provided, how it is provided and where and when it is provided.

— Stronger links between education systems and the labour market, and better systems for translating labour market signals into educational choices.

— Wider access to learning throughout all stages of life, often by those who have been away from formal learning for many years.

— Wider access to learning by groups who are under-confident in, unskilled in, or unused to negotiating access to, complex learning systems. If such individuals are to have wider access to learning, many will need to have access to the information and advice required to make it possible.

Within the labour market, well-organised career information, guidance and counselling can: Improve the accuracy and accessibility of the information available to individuals about short- and long-term job opportunities. In turn this can improve individual decision making about jobs and about job training opportunities, and improve the allocation of human talents within the labour market. In particular, well-organised career information, guidance and counselling can help to:

— Achieve a better match between skills, interests and qualifications on the one hand and available job opportunities on the other; and

— Unearth the talents of those who are not favoured by life's circumstances, thus improving the social and intergenerational mobility of talent.

— Help to improve the allocation of labour across regions, industries and occupations in the face of labour supply and demand fluctuations resulting from technological and structural change; and - Make a key difference between the successful and unsuccessful implementation of active labour market programmes and active welfare-to-work programmes (together with other support services).

These roles for career information, guidance and counselling services becomes increasingly relevant as human knowledge and skill come to play an increased role, compared to capital and labour, in national economic performance. They become still more important in the context of discussions about new concepts of careers that emphasise individual responsibility for career management, and individual and corporate responsibility for developing employability skills, often as a substitute for long- term commitment or loyalty.

Differences in institutions and traditions both constrain and provide opportunities in different countries. All countries face choices in the ways that career information, guidance and counselling services can be configured to meet key public goals such as lifelong learning for all and active labour market policies. One way to elaborate upon these options is to develop "scenarios" or "models". These would incorporate a range of dimensions, and of options within each dimension. Possible dimensions for such scenarios, and examples of options within these, might include:

The role of the state

— Direct provider.

— Main funder.

— Residual funding source in areas of market failure.

— Quality assurer.

— The role of the profession and other parties

— Professionally qualified staff act as the principal provider of services.

— Organisations representing professionally qualified staff act as the principal standard setters and quality assurers.

— Substantial service provision occurs through para-professionals such as information officers and subject teachers.

— Substantial service delivery occurs through community members such as parents, employers, alumni and peers.

Governments directly pay for and provide virtually all services, with little contribution by individuals or enterprises. Nearly all service delivery staff are employed by central government organisations. Governments pay for virtually all services, but provide very few directly, with most services being provided under contract by a wide range of decentralised agencies. Governments pay for services to designated target groups-mostly youth, the disadvantaged and those on low incomes-and individuals and enterprises pay for the bulk of other services.

Governments control quality through the qualifications that are required of the staff who they employ to provide services and through the quality implicit in public delivery. o Voluntary standards, developed by professional associations of guidance workers, exist for staff skills/ staff qualifications/service delivery/career information. o Government-developed or

-endorsed standards exist for staff skills/staff qualifications/service delivery/career information and are used as a basis for resource allocation, recruitment decisions and the like.

Most career information is created and disseminated by governments. Governments contract out most of the production of career information, both print and electronic, to private publishers. A large number of private publishers compete to produce and sell print and electronic career information. Government-funded organisations such as schools and employment services are funded to purchase information from their preferred private suppliers.

The production of "league tables" or guides that rank institutions allowing potential students to compare post-secondary educational institutions is common in the private market for career information and is encouraged by governments. Information on salaries, employment rates, vacancy rates and the like is standard in occupational information.

Educational and course information regularly includes information on student destinations, employment rates, earnings and the like. Most of the clients for career guidance services are students and public employment service clients.

The field of career guidance contains a rich literature on theory and practice. In late 2000 the OECD's Education Committee and its Employment, Labour and Social Affairs Committee each endorsed a new activity on policies for career information, guidance and counselling services. This is a fairly new development for the OECD. In the mid 1990s the Centre for Educational Research and Innovation conducted case studies of national approaches to career guidance for youth, and pointed out that recognition of the importance of career guidance was only just beginning to move from the professional literature into the reality of policy.

A recent study has commented briefly upon the roles of personal advisers within welfareto- work programmes and upon the tools that are required for them to do their jobs effectively. However in general the policy issues involved in the organisation, management and delivery of information, guidance and counselling services have not been treated comprehensively in OECD work.

Many individual examples of good practice, information and guidance systems are frequently not well organised in many countries, and have often not been given a sufficient priority by those responsible for youth transition policies. Similar observations have emerged from a current OECD thematic review of adult learning. One purpose of the proposed new activity on information, guidance and counselling services is to follow up these observations. The new activity has, however, wider purposes.

The OECD's current mandate from Education Ministers requires it to explore ways in which lifelong learning for all can be made a reality. In its detailed elaboration, the notion of lifelong learning for all involves more flexible pathways through initial education, easier re-entry mechanisms for adult learners, stronger links between initial education and training and the further education and training of adults, more flexible mechanisms for the recognition of knowledge and skills acquired outside of the classroom, and a more student-centred approach to learning that gives the individual greater control over the content, mode and location of learning.

In turn, all of these require, if they are to become a reality for larger numbers of learners, more effective "learning signposts" in the form of information guidance and counselling services. This brings questions of the organisation and delivery of information, guidance and counselling services to the heart of a key public policy concern. At the same time, many countries have been adopting more active approaches to policies for the unemployed and for welfare recipients: the concept of mutual obligation is becoming more widespread, with the receipt of government income support often being contingent upon the individual developing an individual action plan, in association with a counsellor or adviser, to re-engage in active job search, education or training.

Taken together these developments in education policy, in labour market policy and in welfare policy imply a greatly increased role for information, guidance and counselling services. In short, how can the ways in which career guidance services are shaped help to meet some key public policy objectives? Twenty years ago, if faced with questions such as this, governments would have had few options. Like other personal services such as hairdressing, career guidance had traditionally been delivered largely in a one-to-one, face-to-face mode that provided limited scope for productivity gains.

Twenty years ago governments, confronted with challenges such as those outlined above, would have been faced with a choice of either expanding access to services at substantially increased cost to the public purse, or of keeping costs manageable by setting tight criteria for access. Another option would have been to ration access by price, with major implications for equity and fairness. However over the last two decades, and in particular over the last decade, new techniques and new technologies have provided substantial scope for productivity gains in the delivery of career information and guidance services.

Developments in communications technology, including call centre technology, have opened up new possibilities for telephone information, advice and counselling services. Another way to increase the productivity of careers assistance services is to systematically 4 involve others who are not necessarily career professionals and to make use of their expertise and knowledge. Examples include programmes to bring employers and parents into schools to talk about jobs and careers that they are familiar with, community mentoring programmes, careers fairs that involve many employers, industry associations and educational institutions, and the type of systematic use of alumni that is found in the careers services of Japanese colleges and universities.

All of these developments and approaches require career development professionals to learn new skills and to work in new ways. While these new options and new techniques might be seen by some as a way simply of reducing the cost to government of providing career information and guidance, a much more positive view is to see them as a way of greatly opening up access to career information and guidance without incurring a substantial increase in unit costs.

By themselves they are not a solution to the questions that were posed above about how career information and guidance can assist to implement broad public policy objectives such as the implementation of lifelong learning for all. But they must be an important part of the solution when put into the context of questions about access, quality, financing methods and the like.

The challenge is to draw a comprehensive picture of the organisation, delivery and staffing of career information, guidance and counselling services that includes them as one element in overall strategies to achieve goals such as lifelong learning and active labour market and welfare policies. Within the broad approach that has been outlined above, there are a number of specific issues and questions that will be examined in the new OECD activity on policies for career information and guidance that started late in 2000.

Educational and occupational information that is used in information, guidance and counselling services: how it is produced and by who, how it is targeted to clients, and whether standards exist for it. This asks about the ways in which information, guidance and counselling services are funded; the ways in which costs are shared; and the financial resources devoted to information, guidance and counselling services.

An important feature of the activity is the way in which the OECD is working in close partnership with the career guidance profession and other bodies. The OECD assisted in the organisation of the March 2001 international symposium hosted by the Canadian Career development Foundation, and the European Commission and the OECD will co-operate in the commissioning of consultants' papers for the activity.

2

Integrated Career Information

Over the past decade, many countries have witnessed significant changes in the structure of work and learning. The globalization of markets and the need to remain competitive have led business and industry to seek increased flexibility in their workforces. Workers are increasingly expecting to move back and forth between education/training and work. These shifting expectations are creating greater demand for career information, career counselling and guidance services.

There is much diversity across countries with respect to how these services are organized at the national, provincial or regional and local levels, and what models best meet the need for periodic and lifelong services. But at the local level, many individuals are closely connected to their communities, and these communities have unique local labour markets and opportunity structures. A "one size fits all" information and guidance service would make no practical sense; local approaches and local information are essential.

Lifelong learning sits squarely at the centre of public policy in most OECD countries. For example, successive governments in Canada, the United States and the UK have allocated significant public funds for research, policy development, program design and delivery that support continuous learning among youth and adults. For those countries at least, lifelong learning is on the short list of priorities for 2001 - 2005. Policy makers have promoted lifelong learning over the past two decades as an important route to secure individual and societal welfare. It is an issue around which governments at all levels, community-based organizations, learning institutions, enterprises and unions have coalesced. For business, it is not a social but an economic issue.

Lifelong learning among employees is the key to maintaining currency of skills. Organizations must provide learning opportunities over the span of a career in order to retain and develop valuable people. Lifelong learning becomes a reality when:

— Different kinds of education and training are interconnected, transparent and accessible to the learner (primary, secondary, post-secondary education; classroom, workplace and web-based learning);

— Life and work goals are both served across the life span;

— Individuals, institutions, organizations all have a means to plan and support continuous learning;

— Learning is clearly situated in a career development process; and,

— Learning opportunities are accessible for all workers.

The kinds of skills that form the human capital in a country range from job task specific ones to essential skills that are used both at work and in daily life. The skills needed in a growing knowledge economy change constantly. Clearly, skill development starts in elementary school and extends to people in their retirement years. Meeting skill needs involves all levels of government, public and private education, business, organized labour, the voluntary sector, and all sorts of community interest groups. For individuals, ongoing skill development is a key ingredient of career development.

Trends in Career Guidance Services

According to Watts, three major emerging trends appeared in the decade of the 1990's:

— Guidance is being viewed as a continuous process that should start early in schools, continue through the often extended transition period to adult and working life, and should then be accessible throughout adult life;

— A more open professional model is emerging as guidance specialists are expected to apply a range of interventions (e.g. curriculum programs, group work, computers and other media). They are more often working with and through networks of other individuals and agencies (e.g. supporting guidance roles of teachers and supervisors, and involving parents in the guidance process). The personal advisor role within the recent Connexions program in England links guidance specialists more closely to front-line youth workers, and so is an application of a more open and networked professional model; and,

— There is a greater emphasis on the individual as an active agent, rather than a passive recipient, within the guidance process.

There are also clear signs in several European countries of career information and guidance being accorded a higher priority than in the past. This is particularly evident in parts of the UK, especially in Scotland and Wales. Career information and guidance are seen as important measures in the improvement of people's skill levels, and in the full utilization of a country's human resources. The delivery of career information and guidance services is also becoming deregulated.

In a few countries there has even been some limited application of market and/or quasi-market principles. For example, in the UK, many responsibilities of the Employment Department for training and guidance have been devolved to Learning and Skills Councils (LSC's). In France, the inter-institutional skills assessment centres (CIBC's) derive their income from assessments they carry out, with explicit costing and the threat of closure if they fail to attract clients.

In the Netherlands, more autonomy was given to schools to determine their own guidance structures within national guidelines. The Advisory Offices on Education and Employment (AOB's) offer services to schools, to the Manpower Service Organization, and to employers on a contractual basis. Decentralization of service delivery has occurred to some extent in most countries. In Denmark, most initiatives are taken at the regional or local level. Just a few years ago in France, all guidance organizations were run by the central government. Now a large number of initiatives and services are based on local structures or associations.

In Spain, Autonomous Communities have grown in importance, resulting in a diversification of guidance services. A complementary development is the formation of national councils that bring together a range of bodies directly involved, or with a stake in the delivery of career information and guidance services. Such national councils have been established in Denmark, The Netherlands, Italy and the UK.

In the United States, career information and guidance services are envisioned as an important component of the preparation of students for the world of work. Given its importance, the United States government has provided a legislative basis for federal support to career guidance and counselling in American schools. The first set of federal statutes are contained in the Carl D. Perkins Vocational and Applied Technology Education Act of 1990. The second is contained in the School-to-Work Opportunities Act (STWOA) of 1994.

Both the Perkins Act and STWOA call on state and local agencies to bring together partnerships of educators and businesses to build high quality school-to-work and vocational/technology education programs. Both laws call for professionally licensed and trained counsellors to administer career information and guidance programs. Another major trend in the US is the establishment of standards and professional and technical support in the delivery of career information and guidance services.

There are signs of an increasingly open and networked professional model seen in the certification of both professional Career Counsellors and Career Development Facilitators. Leadership in this area, until 2000, was given by the National Occupational and Information Coordinating Committee (NOICC), and a network of parallel state committees (SOICC's). This was a joint project of several US departments of government including Labor and Education. Career information, Information systems, and Career Development were together.

NOICC has now been replaced by the American Career Resource Network and State Career Resource Networks. In this current structure, there has been a separation between career development which is within the Department of Education while information systems are within Labor.

Privatization and decentralization have become buzz words for all levels of government and almost every government agency in Canada. The method of "outsourcing" and the providers of services may vary, but the result is the same. Fewer social services are being provided directly by government staff, with larger numbers of non-government agencies involved in the service delivery. Career information and guidance services are, in the main, public services, available through educational institutions, provincial and federal departments, and municipal agencies.

Career, employment and outplacement counselling in the private sector have existed for many years, largely on a fee for service basis for those able to pay. But the landscape has changed. Many more private practitioners are providing services under government contracts to a more diverse clientele. Service provision under these agreements continues to be free of charge for the clients.

The largest numbers of practitioners work under the umbrella of not-for-profit community groups. This is also an extremely diverse group with multiple skill sets and diverse professional backgrounds. Public policy in Canada over the past five years or more has emphasized individual responsibility and self-sufficiency or autonomy in career development. Youth and adults are encouraged to independently use the materials and services available through federal, provincial/territorial, or community-based resource or career centres.

All levels of government have poured the lion's share of funding into client self-service. Much of the impetus for self-service comes from government's desire to reduce the cost of services. It is also being driven by the rapid development of Internet technologies offering high levels of interactivity, visual appeal, and even the use of audio communications. Career information can be more efficiently delivered over the Internet in a self-service mode than can career guidance and counselling. Cost-benefit research continues to be needed on the effectiveness of different delivery methods for different clients to provide a foundation for resource allocation.

Client case management is becoming a keystone of the integrated service delivery approach in Canada. Case management aims to ensure continuity and availability of service in a community partnership environment. It helps the client to connect to different services offered by different organizations and to integrate self-service outcomes into the provision of individual assisted services. In its contracting of career information and guidance services, the federal department of government responsible for labour market programs insists on the use by all service providers of a common approach to client management involving their own computerized system.

The use of technology is changing the delivery of career information and guidance. Increasingly, clients are expected and able to do more on their own. Many use computers to explore careers and the world of work. They use self-assessment programs that help them to evaluate their interests and make occupational choices. Programs are in place to match job-seeker skill sets with available job openings. Very little practitioner intervention may be involved when these systems are used.

The role of the guidance or career development specialist has come under greater scrutiny as a result. Specialists are increasingly being required to provide evidence of the tangible educational, economic and social outcomes of their services.

Career information and guidance services are provided in many different organizations - classrooms, guidance offices, human resources departments, community agencies, private practices, employment agencies. However, it is often difficult for clients to find their way to the right service. Delivery systems at the local level are often neither user-friendly nor transparent. There are at least two major hurdles to overcome:

— *Efficiency* - An efficient system is one where need is matched to the service provided. More work is needed in most countries to map out the types of interventions (i.e. self-service; one-onone; group; peer) that best suit different client needs and to experiment with and evaluate the effectiveness of the different methods;

— *Gaps in service* - In many countries, Canada being one, there is a disconnect between educational departments and labour or employment departments. A seamless service bridging the two often does not exist. As a result, there is no natural transition for school leavers to enter the workforce in terms of where they go for career information and guidance assistance. Help may be available from a community agency, but it is often difficult to find out which one to go to. Government service delivery points frequently have specific criteria to access levels of service other that self-serve (being an employment insurance recipient for example). These criteria can create access barriers and result in service gaps.

The experiences to date of many countries would suggest that the collaborative interactions of many players or stakeholders are necessary to create a coherent career information and guidance service delivery system. These interactions need to occur at the national, regional and local levels. In a coherent system, the interactions between stakeholders would tend to complement each other. In an incoherent one, the individual is confused, and this often leads to an inefficient allocation of resources, both human and financial.

Countries need to identify the stakeholders in the design and delivery of career information and guidance services, determine the potential roles of each, and establish a mechanism(s) for bringing the stakeholders together to develop or improve the system.

Programmes and Policies of Career Guidance

To provide coherence and integration, many countries have centralized their career information and guidance policies, programs and services under one or two government departments. In the UK for example, two government departments are largely responsible for the provision of career information and guidance services - the Department for Education and Skills and the

Department for Work and Pensions. Canada and the United States have taken a contrasting route.

Canada's alternatives for bringing coherence to the overall system, and for integrating different service elements, have included: collaboration of the various players involved through labour market boards; better connecting diverse services through local service delivery networks; and developing complementary policies and services at the national and provincial government levels.

Building collaborative and complementary career information and guidance services requires strong leadership. In Canada and the United States, career and labour market information has become a shared role of their federal, provincial and state governments while guidance and career development services have become the primary responsibility of the provincial or state governments.

For example, the United States established (early 1990's) a legislative base for federal support to career information and guidance. Both the Carl D. Perkins Vocational and Applied Technology Education Act of 1990, and the School-to-Work Opportunities Act (STWOA) of 1994, are designed to respond to the critical need to prepare young people for the world of work and to make the workforce more competitive. The purpose of the STWOA is to establish school-to-work systems that bring together partnerships of educators and businesses to build quality programs.

It is designed to provide all students -not just students in vocational and technical education programs - with the opportunity for work-based learning experiences. The Perkins Act sets the direction for state and local agencies as they develop vocational and applied technology education programs to equip youth and adults with the academic and technical skills needed in today's and tomorrow's labour market. Both laws include explicit guidance provisions.

The STOWA legislation encourages states to employ various approaches to developing and implementing school-to-work opportunities programs. These include school-based learning, work-based learning, and connecting activities. It requires states to provide professionally licensed and trained counsellors to administer career guidance and counselling components. The Perkins Act requires that each state provides assurances it will provide leadership, supervision, and resources for comprehensive career guidance and vocational counselling. It stipulates that states must make career and guidance programs equally accessible to students from special populations.

State programs must also include professional development activities for teachers and counsellors working with vocational education students and community-based organizations. More recently, the United States enacted (1998) the Workforce Investment Act. This act reforms federal employment, adult education, and vocational rehabilitation programs to create an integrated, "one-stop" system of workforce investment and education activities for adults and youth.

Organizations/agencies that carry out post-secondary vocational and technical education activities are mandatory partners in this one-stop delivery system. The WIA is administered by the Employment and Training Administration of the US Department of Labor. Federal funding is available under the Perkins Act, STOWA and WIA to states, and through the states to local agencies that design and implement initiatives. "Core indicators" that are similar for the three programs are used to measure state and local performance.

The European Commission's White Paper on education and training (European Commission, 1995) was part of a process to simultaneously provide analysis and to put forward guidelines for action in the fields of education and training. The paper sets out the action to be taken in the member states, and the support measures to be introduced at the European Community level. Given the diversity of national situations and the inadequacy of global solutions, the paper does not propose a single model for education and training in the EU. Rather, it provides suggestions and guidelines intended to support and supplement policies and programs devised by the national, regional and local authorities. The paper clearly states the importance of promoting access to education and training.

One of the necessary conditions for access is adequate information and guidance. According to the Commission, the citizen of Europe has better information when choosing a hotel or a restaurant than when choosing a type of training. To provide better career information and guidance, the paper suggests that member states set up "knowledge resource centres". It further advocates the establishment of "external cooperation networks". These centres and networks are seen as the outcome of local cooperation between research institutes, companies and teaching establishments.

At the national level in Europe, many countries have created labour market boards or councils. These boards or councils were first established at the national level, and then later were propagated at the local community level. It has already been mentioned that career information and guidance services councils are well established in Denmark, The Netherlands, Italy and the UK. These national and local councils are responsible, among many other things, for the inclusion of quality career information and guidance in labour market transition programs.

National governments made the decision to use boards or councils for the development and administration of labour market policies, programs and services. National policy and funding supports the boards and councils. In almost all cases, partnership arrangements at the local level are encouraged as the primary delivery mechanism for programs and services. For example, in the UK there are currently 76 partnership arrangements for the provision of career information and guidance to adults.

Historically, the federal government has had primary responsibility for labour market matters. Over the past several years federal responsibilities have been handed over to some of the provinces though Labour Market Development Agreements (LMDA's). Five provinces have taken on the delivery of all career development services except for the provision of labour market information (LMI). Four provinces co-deliver the services with the federal department responsible for labour market matters, Human Resources Development Canada (HRDC).

Many of the services have been outsourced to the private (notfor-profit and for-profit) sector. The only universal service is access to LMI. Entitlement to services such as career or employment counselling, skills upgrading, and re-training varies by province/territory. Job placement is almost entirely left to the private marketplace except for the provision by the federal or provincial governments of self-serve job banks. The governments got out of the job placement business mainly because their placement services were not broadly used by employers. The self-serve job banks were, however, well patronized by employers and job seekers.

It is important to note that the devolution of labour market programs and services to the provinces/territories was the subject of considerable public debate, with all communities of interest (business, organized labour, education/training, employment equity groups) having had their say. In Canada's highly decentralized system, it is difficult to align policies, programs and delivery mechanisms around countrywide priorities such as lifelong learning, skill development, use of technology, and active measures for unemployment and welfare clients.

To arrive at common and less fragmented views and approaches to career development services, intergovernmental bodies have been established such as the Council of Ministers of Education - Canada (CMEC) and the Forum of Labour Market Ministers (FLMM). Canada's national approach to decentralized service delivery also includes the use of economic sector organizations. Both the federal and a number of provincial/territorial governments are collaborating in the establishment of sector-wide organizations mandated to develop and implement career development and training initiatives.

The governments provide all or some of the funding for the organizations. Industry provides some funding and expertise. The sectoral organizations try to establish partnerships at the local community level for the delivery of initiatives created by their organizations. Their role in career information and guidance has mostly focused on the development and dissemination of career information specific to their sector. But they have traditionally had difficulty in doing this. For one thing, they are often not well connected to the community and volunteer organizations that work with youth.

And the educational system is so inundated with information they do not always react positively to the provision of more information from national or provincial sector organizations. The Canada Career Consortium, a national partnership of career development community members including Sector Councils and funded by HRDC, is playing a facilitating role in co-ordinating and developing strategic implementation strategies to make sectoral materials available and used locally.

Canada has maintained the tradition of providing guidance and counselling services in secondary schools. Guidance counsellors, who are qualified teachers and guidance specialists provide a full range of counselling and crisis intervention services as well as career and post-secondary planning. Sheer student case-loads mean that not every student has access to a counsellor. In spite of the introduction of government and private sector policies and programs aimed at encouraging youth to enter the trades and technology, students who are not post-secondary oriented tend to receive little guidance.

In the Province of Quebec a somewhat different approach was taken. In Quebec's case, the decision to move to a new preventive policy model was suggested by the Professional Order of Quebec Guidance Counsellors at a general forum on education. There was consensus among career development practitioners and policy makers to introduce a new approach on an experimental basis. Funding over four years was provided to implement the "école orientante" (the guidance-oriented school).

The guidance-oriented school is the creation of an educational environment where everyone is concerned with:

— Helping students understand why they are learning languages, maths, sciences, and so on;

— Giving students a coherent message about the usefulness of their present studies; and,

— Providing students with personal experiences enabling them to build their own identity, work experiences and meaningful contacts with the labour market, and obtain information about what is available (jobs, careers, training, etc.). Increasingly, there are efforts to place career education into mainstream curriculum.

Coherent, integrated career information and guidance services can be seen to exist in many countries at one or more of three levels:

— National level;

— Regional/state/provincial level; and,

— Local/community level.

Policies and approaches are important to the development of regional and/or local level service integration. The integration of career information and guidance services into a coherent, and possibly a seamless, service delivery structure at one or more of the three levels typically occurs within the wider context of the delivery of employment, education, training, and other social services.

It is also possible to find examples of integrated service delivery of career information and guidance services for one group of clientele and not for another. In some countries, integrated services at the local level exist for youth in secondary and post-secondary school, but not necessarily for adults. Sometimes integration is achieved for both youth and adults in transition, but not for people across the entire life span. In looking at examples of what works for the integrated delivery of services it will be made clear whether the initiatives apply to just youth, or adults, or if it exists for people across the life span.

Finally, it should be understood that there are different types and degrees of integration among organizations that provide career information and guidance services in a country. A continuum of types or degrees exists. For simplicity, four types of integration are demonstrated in the examples that follow. They are, from the least to the highest degree of integration:

— Information sharing, networking and possibly staff exchanges (network model);

— Co-location of services where the organizations share premises but retain separate staff, their own funding, and distinct boards of directors (or advisory councils) (co-location model);

— Single points of service where the organizations share premises and staff, where they may combine their funding sources, but they retain separate organizational mandates and boards of directors (or advisory councils) (one stop model); and,

— All services organized under a single organization and governed by a department of government, or single board of directors/advisory council (full integration model).

Cooperative Education and Apprenticeship Programs

In many OECD countries, employers, unions and the schools are all realizing that there is too little about the world of work in the schools, and too few contacts with students in the workplace. Cooperative education, work experience, and apprenticeship programs are intended to provide a bridge between school (or learning) and work. Apprenticeship and work experience programs are broader initiatives that should, and usually do, have an important career information and guidance component. Within the wider program, the career information and guidance component may be fully integrated across the national, regional and local levels, or it may be integrated only at the regional or local levels.

Many European countries have a dual-track education system. Both Denmark and Germany have systems for preparing youth for work that are an integral part of the educational and adult training systems. Following ten years of compulsory education, almost all youth in these countries participate in two or three-year apprenticeships, attend technical school, or receive a free university education. These systems are quite transparent, with pathway entrance requirements, procedures, and outcomes that are clear and well-known to students, parents, teachers, workers, and employers.

The various youth apprenticeship programs that students may attend run for different periods on different schedules and with different curricula, yet they are all linked together into a coherent system that is governed by common rules and requirements. Employers express confidence that apprentices, regardless of the school they attend or the firm in which they apprentice, gain a high level of skill and a good attitude toward work.

This systemic approach to providing career information, vocational guidance and training contrasts sharply with the wide variety of programs to which youth in other OECD countries have access, most of which have different entrance and exit requirements and about which little is known in terms of student outcomes. The transparency of the Danish and German systems enables everyone - parents, teachers, students, employees, and employers - to understand the choices available and the ways to follow a given pathway. Students, too, understand fully the linkages among their school performance, their future choices, their ability to learn skills, and their chances of obtaining good jobs. The Danish and German apprenticeship systems, with their guidance components, are examples of a full integration model.

Some Canadian provinces have actively promoted cooperative education and work experience programs in the secondary school curriculum. In some cases, a career development component is attached to the program (e.g. career information exploration; career counselling before and after a work experience). A significant percentage of colleges and universities have cooperative education programs that form part of the requirements for specific programs (e.g. engineering).

Business and industry associations in Canada have long supported an expansion of cooperative education programs. But at the practical level, cooperative education coordinators in the secondary schools often find it difficult to get placements with employers for their students. Employers sometimes cite, as reasons for their inability to offer placements, health and safety regulations or union objections to the use of unpaid student help. Approaches, such as the use of intermediary or brokerage organizations, need to be found to help employers and unions supply cooperative education work placements for students.

Public sector budget cuts over the past number of years have also led to a significant reduction in the number of school staff assigned to coordination of the cooperative education program. In response to overall staff reductions, schools have expanded the role of parents in education, for example through voluntary teaching assistant programs. A greater role for parents in connecting education with work is a possibility yet to be fully exploited by Canadian schools. The Canadian experiences with cooperative education and work experience programs demonstrate the provision of national or provincial leadership and funding for resource development, but with the actual delivery of information and guidance services made available at the local level and effectively tailored for local community applications. This is an example of the network model for type and degree of integration.

In looking at the Canadian cooperative education and work experience programs, it is also evident that career development researchers should play an important role in demonstrating the contribution of viable cooperative education programs to the achievement of mandated curriculum requirements in the schools, and to the readiness of youth for work.

Employer-Based Career Guidance Initiatives

There are many examples across Canada of business and industry setting up special career information and guidance experiences for elementary and high school students. One is in the automotive industry. For example, General Motors uses an interactive distance learning network program to train technicians in dealerships. The company uses the same system to hold seminars for high school class groups, parents and guidance counsellors. The sessions are typically held in the evening at various local dealerships. The distance learning network is used for a video presentation, questions and answers followed by a tour of the dealership.

Even in the absence of the distance learning system, groups of students are invited to dealerships as part of a curriculum-based learning experience. The students are exposed to all aspects of the operation, and complete an assignment on something like "how different parts of the industry relate to one another". Free tickets to an auto show are often given out as an incentive for attendance. This is an example of the network model for integrated services. It is also a career information and guidance services initiative undertaken in isolation, and not part of a wider services integration initiative. It is an important example, as well, of the role in career information and guidance that can be played by employers.

Building Local Networks

Developing local networks among schools, community organizations, labour, and employers is critical to the success of school-to-work systems. The Kalamazoo Valley Consortium Education for Employment Program (EFE) is a county-wide school-to-work system in Michigan that uses a number of strategies to build business-education partnerships for the benefit of in-school youth. At the beginning of their efforts, EFE organized an Education for Employment Outcomes Task Force to identify the workplace know-how skills expected by employers in the local labour market.

The Task Force allowed employers, educators, and intermediary organizations to meet and discuss their needs and expectations regarding the school-to-work transition system for the community's youth. The system continually engages representatives from business and industry through EFE advisory committees, which are organized around occupational areas. The committees meet at least twice during the school year, helping to develop a wide range of work-based learning opportunities.

Local corporations, non-profit organizations, and government agencies have worked with EFE to develop work-based learning programs, offering students formal classwork in worksite settings. The partners work together to develop curricula and on-the-job training experiences, and the business provides classroom space. Business partners also offer paid work experiences in students' occupational areas of interest, and some formal apprenticeships.

Employers in Kalamazoo point to several key factors that have contributed to the success of EFE business partnerships: logistical support provided by EFE staff; mutual respect between representatives from business and educators; personal commitment to EFE by businesses in time and resources; the willingness of EFE staff to grant business-led advisory committees a substantial leadership role; the hiring of instructors and school-to-work coordinators with relevant business background; and a network among EFE administrators and business leaders. This is an example of the network model of service delivery integration at the local level.

A further Canadian "network model" for relating education and work is Applications of Working and Learning (AWAL). This is a professional development activity for secondary school teachers developed in British Columbia with joint funding from the British Columbia Ministry of Education and a federal department of government (Human Resources Development Canada). It has also been adopted in the province of New Brunswick. In AWAL:

— Teachers visit a worksite;
— They talk with management and with an employee about one particular job, using a questionnaire that helps them obtain information about the use of the essential skills and other characteristics of the workplace;
— They develop hands-on learning activities that they could use in their classroom to develop one or more of the essential skills, inspired by the real world application of these skills; and,
— Classroom activity ideas are put on the Internet at the AWAL site to make them available to other teachers.

One of the keys to success of this local level initiative is the provision of funding from the national and regional (provincial) levels, and the built-in mechanisms for networking between school teachers and employers, and among school teachers themselves.

Role of Parents

Parents play a key role in the development of career opportunities for youth by providing support and working with counsellors, teachers, and employers. Parents and guardians who become engaged in school-to-work systems not only improve the future prospects of their children, they also contribute valuable insight to school-to-work partnerships and can serve as community advocates for a school-to- work transition system. Social and economic changes in the structures of contemporary families and workplaces often constrain the time and effort parents can devote to the educational and career development of their children.

Across the United States, practitioners are applying various strategies to overcome these barriers to parent involvement in school-to-work. For example, in the spring of 1994, American College Testing (ACT) and the National Career Development Association released Realizing the Dream, an innovative program for involving parents in their teenagers' educational and career planning. Realizing the Dream contains the resources necessary for a school or community organization to introduce the program during a two-hour workshop, including leader's materials and guides for parents and students.

As well, local program operators have used several techniques to provide parents with information about school-to-work, including publishing brochures and inviting parents to attend informational meetings, orientations, and workshops. Several school-to-work initiatives have contracted with family resource hotlines, which parents and employers can call for advice and information on education-related issues. In addition, on-line connections to resources and organizations that provide support for families on educational issues offer easy access to a wealth of information.

Many school-to-work systems require that parents co-sign training agreements, a step which initiates communication between parents and employers. Some parents take the next step, actually visiting worksites and conferring with employers and supervisors to gain firsthand information with which to encourage and support their children.

Promoting parent involvement in advisory committees and governance structures is essential. School-to-work should operate as a community-wide effort, recognizing that parents bring invaluable perspectives to the partnerships that guide local systems. Parents who serve on governing bodies speak with informed voices regarding the experiences of their children in school-to-work. They are in a position to advocate and work for better information, services, and other resources for their children, and to become leaders and catalysts for other parents.

Labour Unions in School-to-Work Systems

Labour unions are most effective in a school-to-work system when viewed as catalysts for program development and not as special interests that must be recognized. As a result, it is critical that organized labour be involved in a school-to-work initiative from the very beginning. Often, employers and schools collaborate to develop a school-to-work structure, recruiting labour unions to sign on only after a framework has been developed.

Labour unions, however, can play crucial roles in the initial planning and development stages of a program through their strong working relationships with employers and experience in working with employers to develop on-the-job training programs. These existing partnerships and experiences can assist in recruiting employers for participation. Some schools, for example, have reached out to unions first, allowing labour to make the first contact in recruiting employers for participation in a school-to-work system. This is also an example of the network model for the provision of career information and guidance services at the local level within the context of a broader labour market transition program.

Capacity Building in Career Information and Guidance Services

Capacity building is an ongoing process for individuals and for communities. Just as individuals must develop their self-esteem, confidence and skills to succeed in the economy, so too must a community. Often, community is thought of geographically. However, communities are also defined as communities of interest, joined by the need to take collective action to find solutions to shared problems. With respect to career and guidance services, community capacity building is a grassroots process by which communities organize and plan together to reduce poverty, increase literacy, create employment and economic and learning opportunities in order to achieve social, economic and cultural goals.

Career information and guidance services, as well as other roles related to helping individuals access education, training, and work, are linked to community capacity building in a very substantive way. The community's role is to embrace collective processes such as community planning and collective skill building. The goal is to prepare the community at large as well as individuals for an often unknown and/or underdeveloped community-based labour market. A community-based labour market frequently differs from a traditional industrial-based labour market in that much available work exists outside of the formal economy.

Making career connections for individuals is more complicated in this type of market and is closely tied to community planning and 22 priority setting. Normally, these two roles - that of career counselling and that of community planner/developer - are not connected. Bringing community and economic planners and developers together with career information and guidance specialists in new organizations for the design and delivery of services leads to some new roles for career practitioners and community leaders alike. It opens up new possibilities for connecting school and work and identifying and developing opportunites within local labour markets.

In Argentena, for 11 years an agreement has been in place between the Psychology Faculty of the Buenos Aires University and a local county for the development of a program for the community. The general approach is to support youth through collaboration between the University and local town councils. Organizational agreements are reached that aim to:

— Develop psycho-social programs for yoing people, children and families that are delivered in educational centres offering technical assistance;

— Provide teacher and guidance assistant training; and,

— Conduct applied research on community capacity building and career development. The southern belt of Greater Buenos Aires has a high population density. Originally, the whole suburban area formed an industrial region. Over the last decade it experienced an abrupt decrease in permanent jobs and the sudden closure of many companies. Increasing unemployment, sub-employment and unstable labour conditions now affect mainly women and young people. These conditions narrow expectations for the future and affect individuals' personal identities.

Intervention activities are focused on vocational and occupational guidance in order to help young people to develop personal projects for their life, studies, and work. Activities are carried out at town councils, in local social clubs, and in schools. Efforts are made to develop ad-hoc methods and techniques that may actually help, and assess their effects. A "Reflection Workshop on Vocational Guidance" has been created where young people, under the coordination of a psychologist or teacher, are able to reflect and talk among peers about their vocational and transitional conditions, what they intend to do in the future, and about their expectations and personal interests.

Possible jobs, activities, and roles they may expect are carefully reviewed. The purpose is to develop self-confidence and promote actual trust in their capabilities, to widen current alternatives and activity fields by conceiving innovative projects and strategies, and to acquire new tools to face transitional conditions in restrictive, marginalizing contexts such as poverty, unemployment or unstable jobs. Programs are targeted at elementary and high-school counsellors, and kindergartens that are located in the poorest neighbourhoods, working with care givers and parents.

In countries that suffer from prevailing poverty and marginalization, attitudes emerge that tend to "naturalize" such conditions. While some processes create vulnerability, some protective aspects facilitate resilience which is the ability to face adversity. The resilience comes from the people, institutions and the community. To date, it has been observed that the co-location of services model increases community capabilities to develop life-work projects, helps people plan careers, and develops individual and community resiliency.

In 1992, the province of Newfoundland and Labrador, Canada, was delivered a devastating blow when a moratorium was placed on cod fishing. The cod defined life for Newfoundlanders; it was the reason people first came from the old world to fish on a seasonal basis before returning to Europe. Newfoundlanders had not only their source of employment taken from them but also lost a way of life. The atmosphere in the schools with respect to opportunities for youth became dismal. Youth and adults believed they would have to leave the province to have a sustainable future. The provincial government set to work to develop a plan that would assist rural and remote areas of the province deal with this crisis.

The Regional Economic Development and School Initiative (REDAS) was the result of a creative collaboration between a guidance and career development specialist and an economist who determined to find a means to assist youth to become aware of the potential for work opportunities in their own regions or communities. The challenges of bringing practical career education into the schools are common to many countries. Chief among these are:

— If not mandated as part of the regular curriculum, career education components would not be delivered by teachers. But the only way to reach all students is though classroom teachers; and,

— Teachers are subject matter experts. Most have limited if any expertise in career development, economic development and labour market analysis.

European Commission (EU) support program for Northern Ireland began in 1996 with the aim of reinforcing the peace process. A special feature of this program was the appointment of several NGOs as Intermediary Funding Bodies.. One such organisation, EGSA, has long been established as a core provider of information, advice and guidance for adults and holds as a core value a fundamental belief in the liberating value of adult education.

Through the course of this work, EGSA laid the foundations for an Information, Advice and Guidance (IAG) Network at the community level bringing together all organizations which may have an interest in helping adults to access learning. These included careers services, libraries, adult education, and community-based agencies. Collectively they targeted bringing learning opportunities to:

— Those unemployed for a long time;

— Those with low levels of basic skills;

— Rural adults with poor access to education and employment;

— Ex-prisoners; and,

— Women isolated in the home.

The following community development principles were implemented:

— Bottom-up approach in which local people define needs and methods;

— Strong emphasis on capacity building and personal control;

— Sustainability for the community;

— Nurturing the weakest groups, not the easiest; and,
— Equality of opportunity.

Informal methods were used to attract people back to education. Guidance is a specialization and, at the same time, is part of the service provision of many other social service professionals such as adult educators and social workers. The challenge is to develop a sizeable and inclusive community of guidance providers while at the same time safeguarding the appropriate professional preparation and qualifications. There is a need to examine the credentials required for different levels and kinds of services, and to balance the need to sustain the standards of the profession with protective over-professionalizing, since the latter usually creates barriers to service access.

Career Circuit is an example of the importance of not creating barriers to service access. It is a national Canadian initiative geared to strengthening partnership and capacity within the youth career services sector. Not-for-profit community-based agencies provide a large proportion of guidance and career services for out-of-school youth and young adults. Traditionally, the non-profit sector has been fragmented, under-resourced and has had limited access to structures and supports such as professional training.

In US, the role of the federal government has been to encourage the enhancement of employment and related social services by awarding competitive one-stop planning and implementation grants to the states. While the federal government established basic design principles, states have the latitude to select the best approach for implementation. With states designing and controlling one-stop services, the extent and nature of services varies from state to state.

Some states combine employment and other social service programs into one administrative unit. Other states have gone beyond this to a full one-stop shop concept, providing employment and social services in one facility with one common staff to reduce service duplication and to improve service access. Four basic design principles have guided one-stop development. These include:

— Universality;

— Customer choice;

— Integrated services; and,

— Accountability.

Universal access aims to provide customers (both job seekers and employers) with easy, or in some cases unrestricted, access to needed information and services. Customer choice aims to give customers the ability to decide which services, including self-help options, are most appropriate for meeting their needs. Integrated services aim to minimize fragmentation, duplication, and resource limitations by encouraging service providers to collaborate in establishing common service functions and by sharing infrastructure.

Accountability aims to shape the evolution of one-stop centres by emphasizing performance driven/outcome-based services. The Centres are viewed not in terms of the program priorities of the individual partners, which vary in terms of target populations and available services, but rather in terms of the needs of the customers as the starting point, and enabling individual customers to navigate the multi-agency system to access comprehensive services responsive to their needs.

Two basic approaches exist for delivering services in one-stop centres. The first approach involves direct access to services, such as the provision of labour market information (LMI) to support a job seeker's career decision making. The second approach involves brokering of services, such as helping job seekers identify and select training opportunities necessary to implement an occupational choice.

There are three levels of service delivery in one-stop centres:

— Self-help services;

— Brief staff-assisted services; and,

— Individual case-management services.

Beginning in 1997, Human Resources Development Canada - HRDC - established a network of labour market information and employment services offices in the city of Etobicoke. The network consisted of a partnership between its offices and six community agencies, all located at strategic sites throughout the community for ease of client access. Their commitment was ambitious:

— To join together in order to deliver seamless services to clients;

— To work in partnership without self-interest or competition;

— To identify gaps in services and to design the services each would continue to provide according to the best skills of its staff;

— To avoid duplication in services; and,

— To partner in marketing services so the community had clarity on who does what and where. The mandate was "to establish a solid community infrastructure, leading to a seamless network of employment services which responds to the needs of residents in this community".

Career information and guidance services are included in service delivery as part of the broader delivery of employment and some social services. Clientele include out-of-school youth and unemployed adults.

Under the Workforce Investment Act (WIA) of 1998, the United States authorized the establishment of a comprehensive workforce improvement program. The WIA is intended to mobilize states and localities to design and implement creative employment programs for current workers, potential employees, and local employers. Because rural schools possess a host of resources that are rarely present in other locally-based institutions, they have a major role to play under the WIA.

Rural schools are well positioned to be central players in the delivery of WIA programs for both youth and adults. For youth, rural schools can provide: enhancement of study skills through after-school tutoring; career exploration, guidance and development; job shadowing, mentorship, and internship programs; and placement in summer employment opportunities. Since WIA areas in many states often encompass a large number of counties, rural adults needing the services of a one-stop employment centre may be physically located too far from such a facility. They are frequently close enough to rural schools to benefit from the provision of services at these locations.

Rural schools have successfully served as centres for the delivery of WIA programs. A key ingredient in this success has been the partnership at the local level of school administrators, communitybased groups, and employers. Under the WIA, youth councils form subgroups of local workforce investment boards. The councils comprise board members with expertise or interest in youth development. Members frequently include representatives of youth-serving organizations, local public housing authorities, Job Corps representatives, parents of youth seeking assistance, persons with recognized experience in youth activities, and youth themselves.

In UK, government policy has purposefully encouraged the development of extensive partnership arrangements for the provision to adults of coherent local career information and guidance services of proven quality. The active engagement of all partners is seen as critical in helping local providers to meet skill needs and to assess and respond to local demand. Responsibility for the partnerships is currently being passed from the central government to new local Learning and Skills Councils (LSC's), which are being established with access to discretionary funding for the support of local initiatives and services.

At present, there are some 76 partnerships for adult information and guidance service provision. Each is typically a county-size or large urban area serving the needs of perhaps one million people. Although the partnership models vary, they include a wide variety of organizations such as the Careers Service, the Employment Service, colleges, universities and libraries, as well as a growing number of voluntary and community organizations. Better links are also being forged with unions and employers, but this is still a challenge for the new councils.

The UK experience demonstrates the value of providing a seamless service where students and clients in transition from school to work or from work or non-work to new work or learning do not fall in the cracks of "no service" because of a lack of affiliation with large institutions. The UK example also shows how the co-location of services and network models can be implemented together to provide services to youth and adults not by one agency but by a community of partners.

Seamless Delivery System

People who seek access to career information and guidance services at the local level should not have to distinguish who provides the service. They should not have to restart the process of receiving information, making career decisions and deciding on an action plan each time they move to a different service delivery agent. Career information and guidance services should be interconnected at the local level in such a way that users find the services to be transparent and coherent - they do not repeat steps nor do they find gaps in the services available. This is the ideal service network that is often not realized in most countries, for two key reasons.

In many countries career services provided under the jurisdiction of the education authority are typically restricted to in-school youth. Some potential system users, such as school graduates or drop-outs no longer in education but not yet attached to the labour force, find it difficult to access any form of service. Services available without charge to adults are often provided only to those eligible for unemployment benefits or social assistance/ welfare.

For the unemployed not in receipt of some form of income assistance, guidance and career information services are far from being transparent. The same can be said for adults with a long attachment to the labour force who suddenly find themselves unemployed for the first time. In a lifelong learning model, transitions between work and learning are the norm. Services provide opportunities for developing successful transition skills as well as workforce preparation and/or education and training decision making. Provision of services is not tied so directly to the education or employment status of the user (e.g. in-school, unemployment insurance recipient). A second reason for a lack of transparency and coherence is sometimes created through deregulation of services and contracting out to third party deliverers in a local community. The deliverers find they must compete for a sustainable client base. This promotes an environment of competition, exclusion and lack of coordination of services. This model may also tend to favour the easiest clients to serve rather than those who are most vulnerable.

The Canadian example in Toronto is one of collaboration rather than competition. Achieving this in a deregulated and competitive community environment is a significant challenge. The three-tier system of service provision provides one model for a community to cooperatively distribute services according to the expertise of the career and guidance providers. It also suggests a model for strategic and transparent service policy development. The education authority might articulate and share policies outlining clearly the parameters of its services and outcomes for students.

Employment and community agencies might similarly articulate and share their policies for clients served, services provided, issues, and programs. Working collaboratively, a seamless policy from elementary school through to retirement could be articulated in order to support access to lifelong learning and skills development and employment. Such an approach would enable the identification of gaps in service for specific clients and communities.

Career and labour market information websites can improve access to information services across the life span for all learners and workers. Future comprehensive evaluations of their effectiveness as learning tools for all students and clients is essential as a base for guiding decisions on balancing human services with information technology. Many countries have come to recognize the contributions of quality guidance and career information services to the development of motivated learners who are productive and committed workers. However, there are many other kinds of services that also contribute to the development of motivated and productive learners and workers.

Many of the stakeholders important to a coherent career information and guidance system may be playing less influential roles than is ideal. Parents may be active catalysts for career development and lifelong learning, but often require information and understanding about how to do so effectively. Their potential contributions remain untapped.

The involvement of employers in career information and guidance services is not extensive. Their participation is important in finding ways to help workers at lower skill and education levels who are not well connected to, or comfortable with, traditional learning environments. It is also important in providing part-time quality work experience for students as well as supporting workers' access to learning and up-skilling opportunities. The contribution of informal workplace learning is not broadly recognized and is underutilized in most career development program approaches.

An emerging role for career information and guidance services professionals is in the development of linkages and partnerships with other professionals in compatible disciplines. Career practitioners are in a good position to coach and mentor, in the area of career information and guidance, other professionals in the social services such as welfare workers. Career and guidance practitioners in this evolving model have to be increasingly visible outside of their agencies and offices and more active at the community level in leadership roles.

Qualifications of Career Information and Guidance Practitioners

If career and guidance professionals are to expand their roles in the provision of services at the local level, their professional training will have to extend well beyond its current scope in most countries. In addition, the profession will be challenged to be more inclusive of other fields whose professionals have significant impact on successful learning and work outcomes but who are not specialists in guidance and career development.

The challenge is one of achieving a delicate balance between inclusiveness (because the need for service is so significant and requires many human resources), and the protection of quality standards in a field that requires specialized competencies for effective results.

Boundaries of competence and ethical practice are critical professional issues. Career and guidance issues are holistic in that life issues and work issues cannot be compartmentalized and isolated. Those working in the field must know the limits of their competence and restrict their services accordingly. They also must regularly obtain supervision with respect to their practice. These issues are challenging ones when broadening the field to be much more inclusive of different levels of professional preparation.

The Canadian Standards include a Code of Ethics to guide service providers in their every day conduct. However, a code of ethics provides directives and not answers. Many issues are complex and the availability of training in ethical practice and policies on boundaries of practice are important to protect the public, practitioner and profession.

The Career Development Facilitator training program in the USA includes a separate module on ethical practice and defining scope of practice. Career Development Facilitators are responsible for seeking the supervision of a Career Counsellor at specified time periods.

Role of ICTs

Information and communication technologies are transforming career information and guidance services, just as they are transforming service delivery in other sectors (e.g. banking and health services). This poses major issues for policy-makers. The evolution of the application of ICT in the field of career information and guidance can be divided into four phases. The first was the mainframe phase, from the mid-1960s to the late 1970s. A number of computer-aided guidance systems were developed which demonstrated the potential of ICT.

But the costs of direct interaction with the computer meant that the only systems which proved widely practicable in cost terms were based on batch processing. The static nature of this process and the feedback delays limited the implementation of such systems. The second was the microcomputer phase, from the early 1980s to the mid-1990s. The advent of the microcomputer made interactive usage much more economical, and also made it easier to develop and market limited software packages; its attractiveness grew as more powerful versions of the personal computer were developed. The result was a substantial growth in the number of computer-aided guidance systems, and in the extent of their usage.

By the 1990s it was difficult to find a guidance service in any developed country which did not make use of such systems. The third was the web phase, in the late 1990s. The advent of the Internet meant that instead of free-standing systems located in career guidance centres, websites could be developed which individuals could access instantly from a wide variety of sites, including their homes. The ease of developing such websites produced a massive increase in their number; the ease of interconnecting them meant that they no longer needed to be viewed as discrete entities.

Rather than perceiving ICT solely as a service from external suppliers, guidance services began to develop their own websites. The fourth is the digital phase, which we are now entering. The hitherto separate "analogue streams" of the computer, the television and the telephone are merging into an integrated "digital river". Individuals are now able to access the Internet not only through their personal computers but also through their televisions and mobile phones. Greatly enhanced bandwidth will shortly enhance its speed and its capacity for transmitting video and audio as well as text.

Across these four phases, three key trends can be discerned. The first is increased accessibility. Whereas initially ICT-based career guidance and information services were available only at a select number of technically-equipped service locations, they are now available not only in most guidance services but also in a vast range of other locations - homes, workplaces, community locations. The second is increased interactivity. In the early stages, resources were developed as separate systems, offering only limited interactivity with users. Now, they are highly interactive not only with users but also with each other and across inter-media boundaries. The third is much more diffused origination.

Whereas the initial computer-aided guidance systems were developed by large organisations with substantial resources at their disposal, anyone can now develop their own website. Existing European ICT-based resources in the field of career information and guidance have been classified by Offer in relation to the DOTS model developed by Law & Watts: self awareness; opportunity awareness; decision learning; and transition learning. Resources concerned with self awareness are designed to help users to assess themselves and to develop a profile in terms which can be related to learning and work opportunities. These resources range from simple-self assessment questionnaires to psychometric tests; they also include more open-ended "brainstorming" approaches.

Resources concerned with opportunity awareness include databases of learning and/or work opportunities, with a menu of search criteria which enable users to find data relevant to their needs. The databases may cover: education/training institutions or courses; occupations, employers, or job vacancies; voluntary-work opportunities; and information on how to become self-employed. Some include relevant labour-market information on supply and demand.

There are also some examples of work simulations which enable users to explore particular occupational areas in an experiential way. Resources concerned with decision learning include matching systems which enable users to relate their personal profiles to relevant learning or work opportunities. The outcome is a list of the opportunities which match the profile most closely. Also included here are content-free decision-making resources designed to help users to explore options in a systematic way, balancing the desirability of particular options against the perceived probability of achieving them.

Finally, resources concerned with transition learning are concerned with helping users to implement their decisions. These may include support in developing action plans, preparing curricula vitae, completing application forms, and preparing for selection interviews; it may also include help in securing funding for learning opportunities or for becoming self-employed. From a policy perspective, it is important to recognise the range of these applications. Policy interventions are often confined to a limited sub-set of this range - databases, for example.

The feasibility of developing ICT-based systems which cover the whole of the guidance process poses the issue of how such resources relate to the role of the counsellor. Traditionally, most guidance services have been built around one-to-one counselling interviews. The models used in such interviews have varied: from diagnostic approaches in which the counsellor has analysed the individual's attributes and made appropriate recommendations, to person-centred approaches in which the counsellor helps clients to explore their perceptions of themselves and of the opportunities open to them, and to reach their own decisions.

In more recent years, however, there has been a move in many countries towards a more open professional model, in which the concept of the counsellor working with individual clients in a psychological vacuum is replaced or supplemented by a more diffuse approach, utilising a more varied range of interventions (e.g. curriculum programmes, group work, and use of ICTbased resources), with a greater emphasis on the individual as an active agent rather than a passive recipient within the guidance process. As part of this, some guidance services have moved away from a service centred on long interviews to an open-access model, with information rooms containing ICT and other resources supported by brief informal interviews, and with long interviews being available as a residual resource to those who need them.

To rationalise such a model, Sampson et al. contend that a screening process is required. They distinguish three levels of service delivery. Individuals who are initially judged to have a high level of readiness for decision-making are referred to self-help services: career resource rooms and websites designed to assist them in selecting, locating, sequencing and using needed resources with little or no staff assistance. Those judged to have a moderate level of readiness are referred to brief staff-assisted services: practitioner-guided use of resources, supplemented by group sessions.

Those with a low level of readiness are referred to individual case-managed services: individual counselling and longer-term group counselling. Estimates of those requiring case-managed services tend to fall between 10% and 50%, depending on the population, with the remainder being divided between those requiring self-help and brief staff-assisted services. A range of readiness assessment measures, using a variety of constructs (e.g. career certainty/indecision, vocational identity, dysfunctional career thoughts), exist to help in the screening process; dimensions such as age, socio-economic status, gender and educational level represent administratively convenient but conceptually inadequate proxies for such measures. The choice of these constructs/dimensions is crucial in planning services.

In addition, however, ICT now has the capacity to take services to individuals who find it difficult to visit such centres - because they live in geographically remote areas, for example, or because they have disabilities or are home-based for other reasons, or because they are occupied during the centre's opening hours. The concept of "distance guidance", by telephone or through the Internet, makes it possible to deliver guidance services to remote locations, with or without direct staff assistance. In addition, some clients may prefer to access services at a distance.

Increasingly, in all fields, consumers want a service to be available when they identify a need for it, with minimum delay and minimum effort: they want it here, and they want it now. They may be willing to undertake visits to dedicated physical centres where this is feasible and is perceived as offering added value, but their decision rules in this respect are becoming more and more discriminating.

These decision rules may be influenced by their preferred learning style. For example, Sampson suggests - using Holland's personality typology - that an "investigative" individual who typically uses independent problem-solving might prefer (and learn more effectively) using the Internet to obtain career resources and services; whereas a "social" individual who typically uses interaction with others in problem-solving might prefer (and learn more effectively) by interacting with counsellors and fellow clients in a career centre.

In these various respects, ICT has the potential to significantly increase access to guidance services, freeing it from constraints of time and space. At the same time, however, there may be restrictions on access to the ICT resources themselves. There is widespread concern that the growth of the Internet is exacerbating inequalities between the information-rich and the information-poor: between industrialised and developing countries; between the rich and poor within each nation; and between those who are technically literate and those who are technically inept.

In the USA, for example, households with incomes of $75,000 and higher are twenty times more likely to have access to the Internet than those at the lowest income levels, and more than nine times as likely to have a computer at home. Growing access to the Internet through the television and telephone is likely to reduce these gaps; libraries and other public information points can also have an important role to play. For the present, though, the gaps remain substantial.

Most computer-aided guidance systems have been designed so that they are capable of being used on a stand-alone basis, without counsellor support. In general, however, most commentators on the use of such systems advocate the benefits of integrating them into more broadly-based guidance services. There are three models for such integration. The first is the supported model, in which the user is seen - usually for a brief period - before and/or after using the system. The second is the incorporated model, in which the system is used within another guidance intervention - within a classroom session, for example, or within a counselling interview, enabling counsellor and client to work with the system side-by-side.

While this latter example can be very fruitful, it also means that, far from reducing the counsellor time required by the client, the system may increase it. The third model is the progressive one, in which the use of the system is preceded and/or followed by other guidance interventions - interviews, group sessions, experience-based approaches like work experience and work shadowing - in a developmental sequence.

Offer & Sampson suggest that career centres' websites can have at least five different purposes. One is as a funnel into their own existing off-line services, aiming to maximise take-up of these services. The second is to act as a diversion, seeking to take the pressure away from these off-line services by diverting users to other, usually web-based resources where their needs can be met. The third is an enhancement of such diversion, seeking to deliver on-line guidance within the site itself. The final two add further enhancements: providing a forum for putting users in contact with others facing similar issues to their own, or with people who may offer help in relation to these issues (e.g. potential career mentors); and providing a source of distance learning programmes in career management skills and related areas.

Most of these purposes are not, of course, mutually exclusive, but the choice and balance between them require strategic decisions to be made, as do the choice of partners for any partnership arrangements. Not only this, but the process of making such decisions can be a valuable opportunity to review the strategic development of the centre as a whole. Many career centres clearly start by simply establishing a presence on the Internet: as Offer puts it, "we're here, because we're here, because we're here". Thereafter, it seems likely that they go through four developmental stages.

— The first is promotional: promoting what the service offers off-line.

— The second is adaptive: delivering some of these services in on-line form.

— The third is innovative: delivering new services on-line which are not possible, or less feasible, off-line - which is where any partnership arrangements may come into play.

— The fourth is synergistic: to intertwine on-line and off-line services in new ways.

Alongside websites, there has been growing interest in the use of telephone helplines in delivering career information and guidance services. The largest telephone helpline service in this field is the Learndirect service in the UK, which was launched in February 1998 and by the end of 2000 had responded to 2.4 million calls. Other more limited helplines have been launched in other countries, including Canada and New Zealand. A comparative analysis of these helplines indicates that some have been promoted essentially as information services; others as career counselling services.

Some are focused primarily on learning or on work; others on career, embracing the two. Some are aimed at young people or adults; others are all-age. Some are separate services based on callcentres; others are integrated in various ways into more broadly-based services. The decisions made about the framing of helplines in these various respects are critical. Included in this is the extent to which the service should be offered at national or at local level.

With Learndirect, the original idea was that calls should be routed to helplines based as locally as possible.

This is the model used, for example, by the UK National Health Service helpline NHS Direct: calls are routed to local callcentres, and are only passed elsewhere when lines are busy; the notion being that, in time, it might become the "gateway" to all local health services. In the case of Learndirect, by contrast, the helpline is offered largely at a national level. This can result in some loss of quality, in terms of access to local knowledge.

Against this needs to be set the consistency of service and of helpline adviser training offered by relatively large-scale operation. Such decisions have a significant influence on the balance between "global" and "local" dimensions in guidance provision. This in turn is critical in determining the level of integration that is possible with face-to-face services.

Technological synergy

A further important issue here is technological synergy. Whereas the Learndirect helpline was originally conceived as a separate service, a Learndirect website has now also been introduced, and increasing attention is being focused on integration between the two. The website includes not only courses and occupations databases, but also a diagnostic package which provides an assessment of skills, interests and values, and connects the results to occupational families. Each page of the website includes a "call me" button which generates a telephone call from a Learndirect adviser.

In principle, it should be possible in future for the adviser to bring up on their screen the caller's work to date - a draft curriculum vitae, for example - and work on it on-line with them. Conversely, more callers could be encouraged to access the website and be supported in doing so. Again, greater use of e-mail should make it possible to sustain contact over a period of time through a mixture of synchronous (e.g. telephone) and asynchronous communications.

The concept of flexible usage of the telephone, website and e-mail, linked with face-to-face facilities, opens up new opportunities for the delivery of career information and guidance. It means that individuals can initially access help in the form which is convenient to them and with which they feel comfortable. Some feel comfortable visiting a careers centre; some do not. Some are more comfortable on the telephone, or on e-mail; some are not.

In the latter case, it needs to be recognised that the relationship can now be sustained in a variety of ways: not only face-to-face but also at a distance; and in the latter terms, both through synchronised communications like the videophone, the telephone and Internet "chat", and also through asynchronous communications like e-mail and voice-mail. The rationale for the relationship model is that career decisions have an important cognitive component, but that they are bound up very closely with people's feelings about themselves, their sense of identity, and their dreams and aspirations.

Accordingly, the individual can best be helped by working in a relationship with another individual who has the skills to enable them to address their distinctive identity. This is a strong tradition within the career guidance field, but has come under attack on two linked grounds: that by placing the relationship at the centre, it cedes too much power to the counsellor; and that because it is so labour-intensive and counsellors are costly, it is not practicable or sustainable as an extensively delivered model. This leaves the alternative view that guidance professionals should see themselves primarily not as counsellors but as managers of guidance resources: managing diverse resources in ways which enable individuals to find the means through which their personal needs can best be met.

In relation to these two models, ICT tends to be viewed as leaning towards the resource-based model. But this is not necessarily the case: certainly ICT does not of itself demand a jettisoning of the relationship model. Indeed, there is a risk that contrasting the two models too starkly may implicitly hold frozen the familiar and established practice of the face-to-face one-to-one interview.

As Tait has pointed out, it is important to understand how technology is now transforming the ways in which human relationships are pursued and managed. Instead of assuming that crucial elements are lost when relationships are mediated by technologies, more attention needs to be paid to how technology is enabling such relationships to be developed and sustained in ways which are released from the constraints of space, time and physical presence.

Constantly lurking beneath professional anxieties about the use of ICT in guidance has been the fear of reductionism: that the use of technology will lead to simplistic, "quick-fix", information-based approaches, in which the human element is marginalised or eliminated. Increasingly, however, it can be used within an integrated approach not only to supplement but also to extend the range of this human element.

The key distinctions now are not simply between human interventions and ICT-based interventions, but between a more complex range of interventions: direct face-to-face counsellor-client interactions, on either a one-to-one or group basis; technically mediated counsellor-client interactions, on either a synchronous or asynchronous basis; and stand-alone ICT-based services in which standardised services can be repeatedly used by different users without additional human resource cost.

An important issue is how these different interventions can be optimally blended in effective service delivery, attending to clients' varied needs and preferred learning styles. This has implications both for the training of counsellors, and for wider public policy. The potential roles of public policy in relation to career information and guidance services are four-fold: legislation, remuneration (i.e. funding), exhortation and regulation.

Legislation is important in some countries in providing the essential base for such services, but is likely to apply to the services as a whole rather than to ICT in particular. The other three roles, however, can apply specifically to the use of ICT in career information and guidance services. Many governments have seemed prepared to offer funding for initiatives involving the use of ICT in this field. Indeed, they have not infrequently seemed more willing to provide funding for such initiatives than for extensions of other forms of service delivery, and also less demanding in seeking evidence of effectiveness.

Systematic evidence of such effects, and whether they involve any reductions in quality of outcomes, is however currently lacking. Indeed, there is some anecdotal evidence that ICT-based services may increase rather than reduce the demand for face-to-face services - and therefore lead to greater frustration if these services are not available. It may also be that the notion of evaluating the relative merits of different models of service delivery - face-to-face, by computer, by telephone and so on - as discrete alternatives is now outdated.

In the past, these have tended to be viewed as alternative means to the same ends, which should accordingly be evaluated in comparative cost-effectiveness terms. Certainly the Internet has fostered the growth of an open market in the field of career information and guidance: anyone anywhere can launch such services. For example, Web-based recruitment agencies are increasingly offering "guidance" or "careers advice" as a "loss leader" The role of the market in relation to ICT in particular is closely linked to its role in relation to career information and guidance in general. The core of the case for public investment in such services is that they represent not only a private good but also a public good, in terms of their contribution both to economic efficiency and to social equity.

Traditionally, such services have often been perceived as part of social-welfare provision. In recent years, efforts have been made in a number of countries to apply market principles to social and economic activities wherever this is feasible. Under this view, public intervention in relation to public goods should be confined to areas where there is market failure. In relation to career information and guidance, the market would seem to be potentially inadequate in three important respects. The first is impartiality. The market tends to respond to the needs of those with most resources at their disposal.

In the field of career information and guidance, therefore, it tends to be drawn to the recruitment interface, and to the needs of employers at that interface. This can both constrain and distort the services that are offered, focusing them around the need to fill the vacancies on offer rather than to meet the individual's needs. This may not be sufficient to fulfil the public interest. Secondly, there may be market failure in terms of investment. This is particularly true in relation to career information, which is not "excludable": individuals are not willing to pay for the collection and provision of information which will subsequently be available to others free of charge.

This suggests that career information services should be provided by the state. On the other hand, it is argued by some that guidance services should not be funded in this way, because they are specific to the individual and therefore are "excludable". It is significant, however, that in practice the only area where a significant market has developed for career guidance services is outplacement counselling, where the employer pays but has no interest in the nature of the outcome; elsewhere it seems to be difficult to commodify guidance in the way that a market with growth potential would require.

In relation to ICT, the argument for the public interest in investment in career information is evident in the number of countries where governments have supported the development and maintenance of databases on educational and occupational opportunities. Such databases can either be made directly accessible to clients, or can be made available for private-sector organisations to package and distribute, whether on a fee basis or not, as a means of assuring the quality of non-government information provision.

In the USA, for example, federal and state funding have for many years supported a network of career information delivery systems, co-ordinated by the National

Occupational Information Co-ordinating Committee. It is also significant, however, that all of the major "maxi" computer-aided guidance systems were developed initially with funding from government or from private foundations. Similarly, Sampson has argued that publicly-supported Internet-based systems allow centralised planning of the resource and service design, increasing the likelihood that different functions will be effectively integrated.

3

Career Guidance: The Skills, Training and Qualifications

Professional training, qualifications and skills were one of the five transversal issues recently discussed at the Second International Symposium on Connecting Career Development with Public Policy. While the focus at the Symposium was on the role of policy makers with respect to this issue, several separate observations on training, qualifications and skills were made. These were:

— Training programmes have not kept pace with the changing career context which service recipients experience; they do not address the diverse career paths and complex labour market that clients encounter.

— There is little policy regarding the need for training programmes to prepare counsellors to effectively use internet resources.

— Training related to helping guidance providers to be more effective in addressing accountability issues is mainly absent.

— Advances in ICT and the concept of lifelong learning appear to be the driving forces behind reforms of training in the very few instances where such reform in occurring.

— Regulation of entry to employment as guidance workers tends to apply to the education sector than to the labour market sector. The private sector of careers services is unregulated in most countries.

— There appears to be little linkage between training institutions and policy makers.

— Few countries have addressed the issue of diversity of qualifications versus the traditional professional qualification model.

A small number of international studies have examined issues relating to the skills, training and qualifications of guidance workers. A similar methodology was used in a comparative study of guidance services in higher education in the European Union. Guidance services were classified by focus and level. Focus related to educational guidance, vocational guidance, and personal guidance. Level referred to first-in-line services (as part of the formal teaching function, e.g. learner support); second-in-line services (as for the first but with some degree of specialisation, e.g. study adviser/counsellor); and third-in-line services (separated from the formal teaching function, and offered by specialists, e.g. career/psychological counsellor).

There was much diversity in training, roles, and qualifications required, varying from little if any training for first-in-line to highly trained and qualified for third-in-line. Specialist career services were the fastest growth area of the guidance field in higher education across

Europe. The issue of professionalism surfaced particularly for three groups—careers advisers, counsellors, and psychotherapists—with boundaries being defined through their relationship to the discipline and profession of psychology.

The new/future skill needs of counsellors identified by European national correspondents were:

— Skills to respond to the increasing diversity in the student body, including diversity among EU students, i.e. multi-cultural and inter-cultural competencies in the broadest sense.

— Skills in preparing clients to select and assess available information from ICT sources.

— Skills to deal with increased numbers of students: brief interviews, brief therapy.

— A holistic approach in terms of guidance services to be provided to students. A study of educational and vocational guidance services in Europe, Educational and Vocational Guidance in the European Community, funded by the European Commission, examined inter alia the changing role of professional guidance services, including the training and qualifications of guidance workers.

Some associations of trainers and practitioners have set out what they consider to be good practice in the curriculum of the initial training of guidance workers. In the USA, for example, the Council for Accreditation of Counselling and Related Educational Programs (CACREP) has established national standards for such training. The Council's position is that all counsellors, regardless of their speciality, should experience curriculum in the area of human growth and development, social and cultural foundations, helping relationships, group work, career and lifestyle development, appraisal, research and program evaluation, and professional orientation.

In Europe there is a nascent coming together of trainers of guidance workers through annual conferences that to date have centred more on the theory and practice of guidance than on training issues. The sixth European Conference of Guidance Trainers was held in Durham, UK, in 2000. The International Association for Educational and Vocational Guidance (IAEVG) is the main international forum for guidance practitioners and trainers. In a content indexing of all articles published in its Bulletin since 1979, only two articles directly focused on counsellor training, one addressing the European dimension in counsellor training and the other discussing training counsellors for work in business and industry.

The IAEVG is currently undertaking a study of the competencies needed by guidance counsellors. The aim is to define a set of competencies required by educational guidance and career services providers in different countries with the aim of developing international qualification standards. Based on a literature review and feed back from the International Steering Committee for the study, a set of core competencies have been identified together with 10 specialisations. The core competencies include:

— Ethical behaviour and professional conduct

— Advocacy and leadership

— Intercultural awareness

— Ability to apply theory and research to practice

— Ability to communicate effectively

— Designing, implementing and evaluating guidance programmes
— Awareness of one's professional limitations
— Ability to use computers
— Ability to co-operate in a team of professionals
— Knowledge of the lifelong career development process.

Training of Guidance Practioners in the Education Sector

Across countries and within the education sector the range of training varies considerably, from five years (France, Portugal) to several weeks (Denmark, Netherlands). The distinguishing feature here is the relationship to psychology and teaching. In France and Portugal the guidance worker possesses the equivalent of a basic degree in psychology plus a two-year postgraduate specialisation in vocational psychology.

In Denmark and the Netherlands the guidance worker is a teacher and has undertaken a short course in guidance. The commonality between those apparent extremes is guidance as learner support, requiring an expert knowledge of the principles of learning and teaching (educational psychology) and the application of this knowledge to educational and vocational decision-making and transitions (vocational psychology). The differences, apart from tradition, relate to the location of the guidance service and other roles that the guidance worker may be called upon to play.

In France the guidance worker is a staff member of the Centre d'Information et Orientation. In Denmark the guidance worker is a staff member of the school and will also undertake subject-teaching duties. The type of training also influences the professional title of the guidance worker. In France the worker possesses the title of conseiller d'orientation psychologue; in Denmark the worker may possess the title of VET counsellor or school and youth guidance educator.

Between the French and Danish examples lies a range of graduate and post-graduate qualifications. In Germany one may choose work science or social science in teacher education, enabling the possessor to provide career-related learning within the school system. In Spain guidance workers may combine first degrees in pedagogy, psycho-pedagogy or psychology with a further two-year specialisation in guidance. Guidance can be also a one-year post-graduate specialisation for persons possessing teaching qualifications in Ireland. The recruitment pool from which guidance workers in education can be drawn varies across countries.

In Slovenia guidance workers are recruited from backgrounds in psychology, pedagogy, social work, special pedagogy, and defectology. This can lead to interdisciplinary enrichment in the guidance services provided. It can also lead to fragmentation of services to the client/consumer, as the focus of guidance and/or the priorities of guidance worker activities will reflect the particular training undertaken and not necessarily respond to client needs.

Very little guidance activity takes place in primary schools. Where it does occur, e.g. Austria, Czech Republic, Denmark, Slovenia, and Spain, it tends to occur at the upper end of primary school. Where primary school completion takes place at age 11/12, very little formal career related learning or guidance takes place before transition to the next stage of schooling. Guidance workers in education are most likely to function as such in second-level/secondary school. Such provision in second-chance schools and for adult participants in education is relatively underdeveloped.

In the absence of guidance workers in such settings, tutors/teachers/trainers provide assistance based on their own experience and without any formal guidance training. In tertiary/higher education, the wide variation of services across countries reflects the wide variation within countries, this reflecting the differing views of guidance within very independent educational institutions. Guidance within tertiary/higher education is provided in diverse mode, carried out by a range of expert and non-expert guidance workers. This is often evident in separate student services for careers, placement, counselling, therapy and health, and tutorial/academic advising. The training and qualifications profile of guidance workers is not as cohesive as in second-level education.

Qualifications in guidance are requirements for employment in the education sector in most countries in primary and second-level schools but not to date in other education settings.

Training of Guidance Practioners in the Labour Market Sector

Training for guidance workers in the labour market sector across countries is generally organised differently from parallel training in the education sector. The duration of training ranges from five years (Finland, Portugal) to several weeks (e.g. Australia, China (Hong Kong), Netherlands). The longer duration of training is related to the professional qualification of psychologist (Finland, Portugal) or guidance counsellor diplomate (Germany). There is a very wide recruitment pool from which guidance workers are drawn. A guidance qualification or a qualification in educational or vocational psychology does not tend to be a requirement.

Training of short duration is given on-the-job, sometimes in an alternance model (e.g. France). Such training is obligatory in France in order for the worker to have the title of conseiller a l'emploi. Additional and/more focused training is often provided, e.g. in Ireland, to personnel working with specific target groups e.g. long-term unemployed, or youth at risk of social exclusion. Training courses of short duration tend to be job-task-focused and non-accredited. The private sector of guidance services is unregulated in most countries in terms of training and qualifications requirements.

Within both education and labour market sectors across countries can be found a range of occupations and roles which support guidance workers in achieving the programme objectives of guidance services. Examples of these are Youth Information Officer (Ireland, Romania), Information Officer (in tertiary/higher education), and Librarian. While many may possess training and qualifications related to information science and/or communications, their support role in the guidance service is learned on the job and without any foundation in educational or vocational psychology.

Given the information explosion arising from the Internet, it is likely that such persons will increasingly play a key role in mediating information for guidance support purposes. Additional and complementary training in educational and vocational psychology and other disciplines will greatly enhance the roles they currently play in the guidance services.

There appears to have been very little systems change in the training and qualifications provided to and required of guidance workers in the past decade, whatever the changes in the content of the training. However, a number of new training programmes have been developed that support a more open professional model of guidance.

The examples below have been piloted through European Union Programmes and Initiatives, and their longer-term impact remains to be seen. - Community Based Guidance Assistance:

— Significant adults and peers in disadvantaged communities and linked professionals, e.g. social and youth workers, have been trained in front-line guidance skills in order to provide guidance to "hard to reach" young people.

— Adult Guidance—Training of Trainers: Managers of adult education learning opportunities have been trained to establish, maintain, market and quality-assure adult educational guidance services.

— Training Youthreach Staff in Front-Line Guidance Skills: Trainers and tutors working with challenging young people in second-chance schools have been trained in basic guidance skills to enable them to work more effectively with such young people. In these pilot projects, training programmes attracted university accreditation in some countries.

The numbers of guidance workers that are being trained nationally appears to be mainly a function of the duration of training but not entirely so. Estimates provided show Denmark topping the league within the countries responding, with 1,000 personnel completing initial training annually. This compares with 50 guidance graduates reported for Germany. In the UK around 370 persons complete initial training annually; however, there has been a major drop in the past three years in applications and registration for initial training and employers are reporting inability to fill vacancies.

The temporary solution used by UK careers services is to recruit unqualified staff and train them internally. This was regarded by all employers as an unsatisfactory solution, as it brought pressure on other staff, on financial resources, and on the quality of the service available to clients. No comparative studies similar to the UK have been undertaken in other countries. Indeed, national statistics of patterns of training applications, registrations, job applications, recruitment and retention of guidance workers are very difficult to come by. This should be an issue of major concern to policy makers in national human resource planning for guidance services in all sectors of the economy.

The most significant difference within countries lies in the degree of prescription of qualifications for employment as a guidance worker in the education and labour market sectors. There is tight regulation in qualification requirements for guidance workers in the education sector, particularly in primary and second-level schools. Tertiary/higher education is much less prescriptive in both careers and academic advising, with guidance training and qualifications requirements varying from none to post-graduate.

Adult educational guidance and guidance in second-chance schools have traditionally been provided by tutors/trainers without any formal guidance training, though this picture is now beginning to change. By contrast there are no guidance training and qualification requirements as pre-entry conditions for employment as a guidance worker in the labour market sector. The wide gap between training and qualification requirements for guidance workers has other potential negative impact. Communication between education and labour market guidance services may suffer, as both speak a different guidance language. Mutual negative perceptions increase.

Both can feel threatened by the others' professional standing. Above all there is little or no occupational mobility for guidance workers between the sectors. Where such flow is possible through recognition of guidance qualifications (e.g. Czech Republic, Ireland, Korea, Luxembourg, Norway, Romania, UK), it tends to be from the education sector to the labour market sector. In many countries there is no mutual recognition of guidance qualifications between the education and labour market sectors. Such recognition and consequent mobility would greatly enhance the development of a seamless guidance provision for clients.

The mobility issue referred to above is further compounded by lack of training and qualifications structures that would enable guidance workers to move from non-professional to professional status. In only two countries in Europe, Ireland (labour market) and UK, is such movement possible at present. Structures facilitate movement from the equivalent of a two-year national certificate to undergraduate or post-graduate diploma levels.

The initiative for developments of this kind has been government-led (UK) or organisation-led. It is significant that progression for guidance workers from nonprofessional to professional status is a non-issue for trainers and professional associations in many countries. The absence of such progression pathways is a major source of frustration to guidance workers whose training has consisted of short non-accredited programmes and to other personnel who have had many years of experience in guidance roles without any training.

Across countries there is wide variation on who decides the content and methodology of initial training for guidance workers:

— by trainers alone: Australia, China (Hong Kong), Finland, Netherlands, Spain, Slovenia

— by the government ministry alone: France

— by trainers and the professional association together: Ireland (Education), Norway

— by trainers and the government ministry together: Austria, Czech Republic, Greece (Education), Luxembourg, Portugal, Romania

— by trainers, professional association and the government ministry together: Belgium fl., Denmark, Germany, Ireland (Labour), UK

— by trainers and local authorities: Italy.

Nine approaches may be used individually or in combination for devising the content and methodology of initial training for guidance workers. These are:

I. Formal job analysis

II. Formal job review of guidance workers

III. Review of guidance training nationally

IV. Review of guidance training internationally

V. Suggestions or prescription by the professional association

VI. Suggestions or prescription by government ministry

VII. Reaction to public demand

VIII. Reaction by trainers to developments in the field of guidance

IX. Reaction by trainers to economic, social and information society developments.

Reactions by trainers, suggestion of government ministries and of professional associations appear to be the main source of shaping and developing the content and method of guidance training. Austria and Finland each combine all nine methods. Germany and Spain use all except suggestions by the professional association and reaction to public demand. Denmark, on the other hand, depends entirely on reactions by the trainers to developments in the field of guidance and to economic, social and information society developments.

In overall terms, trainers play a key role in guidance curriculum development. Trainers themselves, however, are not very well organised. There are no national or international associations of trainers of guidance workers. Trainer membership of national and international associations of guidance workers provides a proxy forum.

Cost of Training

The role of the government ministry is somewhat paradoxical across countries. In the six countries where decisions are left entirely to the trainers, funding is provided by the relevant government ministry (or ministries) with apparently no other input. In France the relevant government ministry decides on content and delivery of training and funds it entirely. The approximate level of government funding support for the initial training of guidance workers is high, with 100% in Finland, France, Germany, Luxembourg, Netherlands, and Norway.

Some governments support a number of student places e.g. Ireland (education), UK, in addition to providing general funding for higher education.. Self-funding by participants is a strong dimension of funding of training in China, Denmark, Ireland (education), Slovenia, Spain and UK. Training programmes are often run on a shoe-string budget by training institutions. EU Programmes and Initiatives are currently a significant source of funding for training programmes in Greece.

Recurrent Training

Recurrent training is provided annually to guidance workers in most countries and participation in general is optional. The participation rate estimates vary from 100% to 10% or less (France, Germany, Luxembourg). Where participation is mandatory (e.g. Finland (Labour), Ireland (Labour), Portugal (Labour)), the relevant government ministry funds the training. Where such training is an option, it is also mainly funded by government and sometimes partly by the trainees and employers (Netherlands). In Argentina recurrent training is funded by guidance workers themselves. Incentives for participation range from salary improvement (Slovenia) to penalty for non-attendance (Finland). In most cases, reward for participation is either accreditation of training (e.g. Netherlands, Romania) or higher grade of membership of the professional association.

ICT and Distance Education

Very little use is made of ICT and Distance Education to deliver initial and/or recurrent training for guidance workers. ICT has been used for initial and recurrent training of guidance workers in Europe. The positive features cited for the use of ICT for training guidance workers are flexibility in terms of time and place of training, cost-efficiency, and uniformity of delivery. In Greece ICT and Distance Education are viewed as a means of increasing the number of training places for guidance workers. The limiting factors cited are that such approaches are not appropriate for group and interpersonal processes (Austria), and do not provide optimal conditions for behaviour shaping (Germany).

Other limiting factors cited are lack of investment (UK), access and hardware problems (Ireland (Labour), Romania), and lack of expertise and experience among trainers to deliver this training approach (Greece). There is a general preference for the traditional model of training involving face-to-face meetings for the purposes of sharing and exchanging ideas and experiences and for networking.

It is clear that the use of ICT and Distance Education for training guidance workers is not a priority or even on the agenda of trainers, professional associations and government ministries in many European countries. Progress in this field requires the commitment of these key actors. Such commitment is currently lacking. The lack of interest of European countries in developing this training modality contrasts with the USA where the Association for Counsellor Education and Supervision developed and adopted guidelines for online instruction in counsellor education.

There appears to be a general unwillingness to examine the potential and experience of ICT and Distance Education for interpersonal and group processes or even to research such processes. The use of older media such as telephone and television for guidance delivery is also unlikely to appear in existing initial training programmes. It is as if training is time-bound by what is currently known about face-to-face interpersonal and group processes, with no thought being given to the psychological and social phenomena of non-face-to-face interaction. Given the apparent lack of recognition of such life and technological phenomena in guidance training in Europe, one could postulate a knock-on effect on how guidance training programmes treat the issue of ICT in delivery of careers information and guidance. There has certainly to be some modelling effect, positive and/or negative.

Countries such as Denmark, France, Germany, Ireland and Netherlands report that much importance is attached in their initial or recurrent training programmes to the use of ICT to deliver careers information and guidance. As to the preparation of guidance workers to work with and through nonprofessionals and the voluntary sector, only two countries, Ireland (adult educational guidance and labour market services) and Greece, cited this as a key aspect in training for guidance workers. In many countries, e.g. Argentina, Czech Republic, Netherlands, Norway, Portugal, Romania, Slovenia and Spain, there appears to be a blind spot on this issue.

The increasing globalisation and internationalisation of education and employment receives more attention in guidance training in Austria, China (Hong-Kong), Denmark, Germany, Netherlands and Norway. It does not feature in training programmes for guidance workers in Belgium fl, Portugal and Slovenia.

ICT is a significant methodology for delivering career information and guidance. Its applications and potential have been well documented elsewhere. It does not yet appear to be attracting a significant time slot in guidance training in many countries. This can partly be explained by resistance to change in traditional methods of guidance, partly by lack of investment in providing the necessary hardware, software and internet connectivity by training institutions and government, and partly by a lack of good models of practice within countries of how the potential of ICT can be harnessed to deliver careers information and guidance.

Guidance is much more than a face-to-face interview. SCAGES (Standing Conference of Associations for Guidance in Educational Settings, UK) identified 11 activities of guidance:

— Informing

— Advising

— Assessing

— Teaching

— Enabling

— Advocating

— Networking

— Feeding back

— Managing
— Innovation/Systems change
— Signposting
— Mentoring
— Sampling work experience or learning tasters
— Following up.

As indicated below, only some of these 15 activities are covered in present quality guidelines or standards: in most cases, the main focus is on Informing and Assessing. Even the more comprehensive quality frameworks, for example the British Guidance Council Quality Standards, do not cover the full range of guidance activities. This leads to the reflection that

— There is room for enhancing the coverage of quality issues in terms of activity areas in guidance
— Some issues/areas are relevant for particular guidance services: few services would cover all 15 areas
— Some issues/areas are left out of scope because they are seen as irrelevant, and/or difficult to measure, and/ or politically sensitive.

In some countries, quality standards in career guidance build on staff performance or skills/competencies indicators, which are generally quite exhaustive. They comprise, e.g., advocacy, publicity, feedback, and quality assurance procedures.

Educational and Occupational Quality

One of the areas of careers guidance in which introducing

quality standards is less complicated, yet still quite comprehensive, is the informational side, which in many cases is predominant in guidance provision. For example, the American NCDA quality guidelines in this area are highly detailed and cover most aspects related to career information services. Several sets of guidelines have been issued by the NCDA, including:

— Guidelines for the Preparation and Evaluation of Career and Occupational Information Literature

— Guidelines for the Use of the Internet for Provision of Career Information and Planning Services

— Guidelines for the Preparation and Evaluation of Video Career Media - Career Software Review Guidelines.

The first of these sets of guidelines acts as a model for the others to some extent. It contains, among its general guidelines, a list of items to help editors of career information: Dating and Revisions, Credits, Accuracy of Information, Format, Vocabulary, Use of Information, Bias and Stereotyping, and Graphics, followed by comprehensive Content Guidelines, all of which contribute to general good editorial performance. Other American standards, focused on web-based career guidance, include standards issued by the National Board for Certified Counselors and, focusing more on the informational side, standards issued by the Association for Computer-Based Systems for Career Information.

Denmark has issued a Declaration of Career Information (with a focus on information on training/educational options), i.e. a list of headings to be covered in all types of career information, regardless of the chosen media:

— Identification (who is imparting what to whom)
— Goal (aims, target group, usage)
— Contents (theme, coverage, style)
— Medium (availability in different formats: hard copy, computerised)
— Structure (organised sequentially or as hypertext)
— Accessibility (computer specification; audio version of printed or computerised material).

The scope for umbrella organisations, governmental and NGOs alike, to issue guidelines on career information, is evident. It provides a relatively easy and cheap area in which to issue quality guidelines. Applying such standards or guidelines, however, is far more difficult, especially in the present versatile and volatile media environment. Standards or guidelines on career information, for good reasons, deal with the tip of the information iceberg, i.e. material produced and designed as career information.

No guidelines address the more clandestine type of information which is imparted every day in, e.g., TV series, sitcoms, documentaries, web-sites, and email-based guidance, in which a multitude of role models are depicted along with more or less biased and distorted information. Thus, the informational aspect of sustaining quality in career guidance and information, which looks relatively simple at first sight, and which is already promoted in some countries by clear guidelines, in fact turns out to be complicated and controversial. And probably impossible to implement in relation to modern integrated media.

Qualifications and Competencies of Staff

In an attempt to secure the overall quality of career guidance, the German Association of Career Counsellors maintains a Directory of Certified Career Counsellors. This directory is seen as important to secure transparency to clients of the formal competencies of guidance practitioners. The Institute of Career Guidance in the UK also now maintains a Register of Guidance Practitioners. This sort of strategic move is paralleled in other, more commercialised guidance cultures, e.g. in the USA where licensing forms a significant part of the path to professionalisation: licensure is an important feature in 44 states.

These regulations are linked with the quality assurance program offered by CACREP (Council for Accreditation of Counseling and Related Educational Programs), whereby the quality of the training and education of professional careers guidance staff is regulated and maintained. This includes a lengthy quality assurance process: direct inspection of the premises, the curriculum, staff qualifications, etc.

People working in career development practice need to demonstrate certain attitudes. They need to be:

- insightful
- honest
- open-minded
- results-oriented.

People working in career development practice need to have certain skills. They need to:

- document client interactions and progress

— accommodate diversity

— collect, analyse and use information

— convey information clearly when speaking and writing.

People working in career development practice need to have certain knowledge. They need to know:

— career development models and theories

— the change process, transition stages, and career cycles

— components of the career planning process

— the major organisations and resources for career development and community services.

All competency areas are important in providing comprehensive career development services. Currently, six main areas of specialisation have been identified:

— Assessment

— Facilitated Individual and Group Learning

— Career Counselling

— Information and Resource Management

— Work Development

— Community Capacity Building

All career development practitioners will need to have a certain number of basic competencies in all six areas of specialisation.

Quality issues in guidance are often linked with other (related) phenomena. One of the links, in recent years, has been a growing interest in the relationship between the social and economic goals of guidance: the effects and effectiveness of guidance have been studied, along with cost-benefit ratios. Few evaluations have considered, specifically, the quality of economic outcomes of guidance itself, although implicit assumptions on the effects and effectiveness of different measures have been made.

One of the difficulties of measuring economic outcomes of guidance is the obvious one that it is very difficult to establish control groups, which are not affected by specific interventions. First of all, it would be morally questionable to deprive certain groups of services which were given to everybody else; and secondly, guidance is difficult to disentangle from other forms of information and inspiration, from the influence of peer advice, the media, and chance, and from other elements of schemes of which they are an integral part.

Potentially, guidance offers benefits to individuals, education and training providers, employers, and governments. Guidance can play a role in fostering efficiency in the allocation of human resources, and social equity in access to educational and vocational opportunities. This is some of the policy rationale behind guidance provision in general. In economic terms, guidance can assist the operation of the labour market in three main ways:

— by supporting individual decisions (labour supply decisions, human capital decisions, and job search decisions)

— by reducing labour market failures (drop-outs from training, mismatch, discouraged workers)

— by contributing to institutional reforms designed to improve the functioning of the labour market (open learning, job-and-training rotation schemes, etc.).

Internationally, some research projects on the economic aspects of guidance have been carried out. But most have experienced considerable methodological difficulties:

— The effects of guidance are not likely to be visible for some time.

— The longer the time that elapses, the more factors other than guidance come into play.

— Controlled trials are the surest method of distinguishing effects from mere consequences. But such trials are difficult to mount, and more so over longer periods: control cannot be indefinitely extended, nor guidance indefinitely denied.

— If the purpose of guidance is to help individuals to clarify and implement their own goals, this makes it difficult to find appropriate standardised criteria against which to evaluate the outcomes.

In short, it is a field with many pitfalls, as OECD has acknowledged. Moreover, the economic value of guidance as such, especially in integrated approaches (educationally based guidance, for instance), is difficult to disentangle from other activities and interventions. On the other hand, guidance is clearly in a number of respects part of an overall attempt to create and obtain benefit from economic growth, the assumption being that economic growth will create more jobs. In this context, guidance is regarded as a cost-effective measure to curb unemployment, which in turn is seen as a waste of human and economic resources.

The economic rationale for a number of specific guidance activities is that they may shorten the periods of unemployment, create greater flexibility in the labour market, or support mobility. In these broad terms, the quality of guidance is linked with its role as a market-economy facilitator, with a supposed economic impact, even if this is seldom in fact measured and documented. With accountability being moved up the agenda in most parts of the public sector, guidance in some EU countries, especially in the UK and the Netherlands, is measured with an economic yardstick: how much does guidance cost, and does it pay? One step further into this concept, guidance itself is put on the market, either through privatisation, or via guidance vouchers, as was the case in the UK as an experiment.

In these terms, a market in guidance itself is created, where, ultimately, non-profitable parts of guidance could be discarded at the expense of more vulnerable users, thus excluding the long-term unemployed and other vulnerable groups, whereas employed individuals would be able to pay for an extended service. In other guidance cultures, such market-oriented developments are not encouraged, or, indeed, seen as signs of quality in guidance.

Historically, there has been a profound interest in many 'developed' countries in measuring guidance, but from different perspectives. During the first half of the 1900s, the interest was linked with the then prevailing psychometric testing tradition, where measurement was the very essence of guidance. Interestingly, this tradition was abandoned in some countries, e.g. Denmark, for a number of reasons, both technical ones, and political ones.

In recent years, evaluations of the public sector have been numerous in many countries, especially in terms of quality assurance exercises. Thus, in terms of guidance, a study on the quality of Danish career guidance, listed a number of generic quality indicators:

- Client-centredness
- accessibility, transparency and coherence of the services
- well trained guidance staff
- valid, precise and comprehensive careers information
- referral to other guidance specialists
- follow-up.

In Europe, one of the purposes of the Single European Market is to increase personal mobility within the European Union. Career guidance may facilitate such mobility: guidance is part of the globalisation process. The boundaryless career is emerging, both physically and metaphorically. Mobility, however, is a coin with two sides: it may improve the quality of life for the mobile, but the processes of mobility tend to leave the immobile behind in poorer conditions.

The negative effects of mobility can include segmentation, segregation and marginalisation. In such manpower exporting areas, the loss of dynamic individuals may add to the cultural and economic downward spiral. In this picture, the role of career development becomes abundantly clear: career guidance/ counselling is a vehicle for economic growth, the irony being that much of the growth is what has been labelled 'job-less growth'. In this capacity, one of its aims is to facilitate personal mobility, i.e. ease the movement of manpower (and students) to economic growth areas, thus serving as a societal lubricant.

Economic growth, in terms of career development, may be sustained by scientifically placing people in their proper occupational position: a testing tradition. Historically, in a reaction to the sometimes rather crude and mechanistic methods of psychometric testing, the client was moved to the centre of career guidance in what became known as the 'client-centred' approach: each individual has a potential of personal growth. The guidance practitioner, in this perspective, is seen as a helper in the process of the individual's self-exploration.

In terms of economic growth, career counselling helps each individual to unfold his/her potential, thus providing a link between personal growth and economic growth. It follows from this brief historic outline that quality issues differ over time, according to the prevailing professional discourse and the societal circumstances.

Applying market-economy principles to careers guidance and information services implies that guidance either acts as a market facilitator (e.g. by helping to balance demand and supply in the labour market), and/or is a market in itself (e.g. by selling career development services at a market price). The counsellor acts as a human capital investment adviser. But the analysis of cost-benefit ratios falls far behind a number of important issues, e.g. care for the underprivileged or environmental concern.

Nonetheless, the International Association of Educational and Vocational Guidance (IAEVG), for example, has adopted a statement on global Ethical Standards, which focus on important humanistic values, and which include a recognition of the tensions between economic growth and environmental issues. In short, new concepts are under way to challenge or supplement the paradigm of economic growth as the basic parameter. The next section depicts some examples of such alternative quality concepts.

Other forms of measuring output and services (including, potentially, career guidance services) could serve as a corrective to the purely economic angle. Thus, Ethical Accounting, a method of describing values, goals and achievements which is used in some companies and educational institutions, could be an additional method in future for measuring the outcomes of career guidance. The economic yardstick is unidimensional; guidance and counselling are multidimensional interventions and need to include ethical considerations.

4

Social Counselling and Guidance

Numerous definitions of counselling exist, but one of the more succinct and helpful descriptions is that by Burks and Stefflre: "Counselling denotes a professional relationship between a trained counsellor and a client.This relationship is usually person-toperson, although it may sometimes involve more than two people. It is designed to help clients understand and clarify their views on their life space, and to learn to reach their self-determined goals through meaningful, well-informed choices and through resolution of problems of an emotional or interpersonal nature."

Counselling may focus on both work related and personal problems, which can include coping with crisis, conflict with others, development of personal insights and improving relationships. Sessions usually last for between 50 and 60 minutes and take place within a confidential setting. Frequency and duration varies, depending on the client's needs, availability and the model of counselling employed.Traditionally, counselling happens face-to-face but alternatives—such as telephone, video-conferencing and online counselling - have emerged in recent years.

Counselling is increasingly recognised as a specific professional discipline, as distinct from the use of counselling skills, which are employed routinely by most health service professionals in the course of their work. It is likely that the area of psychological therapies will become legally regulated within the next few years,with titles such as 'counsellor' and 'psychotherapist' being protected.

The minimum level of training that is generally recognised by the professional bodies for counselling and psychotherapy is a diploma, which includes both theory and practice components. Here are some of the main requirements of professional counselling practice.

Accountability

— Counsellors should be properly trained and experienced for the work they carry out.

— They should belong to a recognised professional body,with a code of professional practice and a complaints procedure.

— Clinical supervision is vital and counsellors should receive at least the minimum level required by their professional body.

Responsibility

— The primary focus of the counselling is the needs of the client.

— Counsellors should avoid situations that give rise to conflicts of interest between their responsibilities to their clients and other parties. This usually means they do not have any other role with their clients.

— Counselling takes place in an appropriate setting that ensures the confidentiality of the relationship between the client and the counsellor.

Workplace Counselling

Workplace counselling is a specialised field,whereby the employer either provides a service or access to one.Over the last decade it has become one of the fastest growing fields within counselling.Most of the growth has taken place in the private rather than public sector,with many large corporate companies now offering this service.

In most cases, the health service has been slower to recognise the benefits for its staff, but in many areas this protected. Counselling for staff can either be provided internally -through a service located in the organisation and by staff employed by the organisation - or externally, where an external provider is contracted to provide the service. Wherever the service is located, thc issue of accountability for counsellors can be complex.

This may be to either the employer or to an intermediate provider, depending on whether the service is provided internally or contracted out. In addition, legal, commercial and health and safety considerations may impinge on the counselling rclationship.Given these complex factors, it is recommended that newly qualified counsellors should not be employed in these settings unless they can be adequately supported and that, ideally, counsellors should have a minimum of three years' post qualification experience.

Staff perceptions of the service's confidentiality are crucial and if employees remain unconvinced, it will not gain the trust necessary to succeed.Whether provided internally or externally, the boundaries between counselling and other functions - such as human resources and occupational health - should be clearly defined. Occasionally staff may be involved in disciplinary processes at work and use the counselling service for support.

However, counselling as described within this guidance should not form part of or be confused with any disciplinary process.Counselling should only be undertaken voluntarily and staff should not be coerced into using the service. Managers and colleagues acting out of concern may suggest contact with a counselling service, but essentially staff should self-refer, free of pressure.

Managers should also be sensitive to the needs of staff using the service, for example in enabling them to use the service during work time, and also respect their right to confidentiality. The following points identify some of the principle features of counselling practice as it applies to the workplace:

— most counselling provision is short-term,with services offering between six and eight sessions, including an initial assessment

— in addition to the minimum professional level qualification of a diploma, counsellors need to be able to work within a short-term counselling framework

— counsellors work with an understanding of the organisational culture—in this case the health service —and of organisational factors which impact on psychological health in the workplace

— counsellors work with an awareness of the interests of different organisational stakeholders and of the potential for conflicts of interest between the needs of the client, the service and other stakeholders.

A range of evidence exists supporting the idea that workplace counselling helps to reduce the level of psychological distress in staff, improves work functioning and lowers absenteeism. For example, the British Association for Counselling and Psychotherapy commissioned a rigorous and independent research review of the evidence to date into the effectiveness of workplace counselling. The results are important pointers to some of the successes within the field of workplace counselling.

Individuals can refer themselves to psychological support at a time of crisis and distress. Acknowledgement of a problem can be the psychological turning point for the individual.Many staff wait too long before accessing help and the availability of immediate psychological support can reduce distress, helping the individual maintain their role at work.

The McLeod study found strong evidence of the individual benefit from workplace counselling, concluding that:"People who make use of workplace counselling typically report high levels of psychological distress, equivalent to that found in out-patient psychiatric populations...Significant benefits for clients can be achieved in three to eight sessions of counselling; only the most severely disturbed clients appear to require long-term counselling help or referral to a specialist service...Counselling interventions are generally effective in alleviating symptoms of anxiety, stress, and depression.Two-thirds of studies have shown that, following counselling, levels of work-related symptoms and stress return to the normal range for more than 50 per cent of clients."

The study by Leeds and Sheffield Universities evaluated two NHS trust staff counselling services, finding a significant reduction in the proportion of clients with significant levels of psychological disturbance. And a study by Cary Cooper into counselling provision in the Post Office found marked reductions in symptoms of depression and anxiety, as well as significant organisational benefits. It is also clear that counselling at work is well received by staff. McLeod states that:"Over 90 per cent of employees who make use of workplace counselling are highly satisfied with the service they have received, would use it again if necessary, and would recommend it to colleagues."

Benefits

The McLeod review also found evidence of very considerable benefits for organisations in having counselling provision. The study concluded that: "Counselling interventions have been found, in the majority of studies to have reduced sickness absence rates in clients by 25-50 per cent. Counselling interventions have a lesser, but still significant, positive impact on job commitment,work function, job satisfaction and substance misuse." The study by Cooper into the Post Office's counselling provision also found evidence of considerable organisational benefits. Cooper found substantial reductions in absence; duration of absence for the six months pre- and post-counselling; reductions in use of other human resources and in frequency and duration of authorised absence; and disciplinary proceedings.

Smewing, in a study of a NHS based Employee Assistance Programme (EAP), found that even staff that had not used the counselling service felt more valued by the organisation, which led to a 'feel good' factor about their employer.

Cost issues are important because counselling provision for staff is essentially competing for resources with other priorities. The more effectively it can demonstrate its value, the more successful it is likely to be in attracting resources. In addition to the Lothian study already cited, McLeod examined a range of studies looking at the cost effectiveness of workplace counselling and EAP provision. His conclusion is that:"Even the most rigorous economic analyses show that workplace counselling and EAPs cover their costs, in terms of economic savings that are generated by employers."

There is strong evidence that counselling has a positive impact on organisational health and a properly targeted intervention will at least pay for itself.However, not all counselling interventions are equally effective and clearly there is a link between service quality and outcomes. Service evaluation is crucial in determining the effectiveness of individual services and how it may be enhanced.

Currently, access to counselling for staff in the health service is far from universal and,where it is provided, is extremely varied in its range and quality. Provision ranges from single - and often part-time - counsellors engaged for limited hours and providing only counselling, to well-resourced services employing a number of staff and providing a range of additional services.The majority of services appear to be either internally provided, or purchased on a contract basis from other health services providers who already have internal provision.

Given that health care is delivered in a range of widely differing settings and by a range of professional and support staff, the manner in which counselling is provided will inevitably need to reflect this. However, in UK, the Royal College of Nursing (RCN) believes that there are some core elements of service provision that should be available for all staff. Counselling is currently provided in two main ways, either face-to-face or by telephone.

Most staff prefer to see a counsellor in person and this should be an essential part of the service provision.However, this may be difficult to provide - for example,where staff are working in remote locations - and in these situations, telephone counselling may be appropriate.The key principle is to ensure that all staff can refer themselves to a quality service. While most services usually offer between six and eight sessions, there should be the option of additional sessions where the counsellor makes a clinical judgement that the client needs extra support.

Counsellors should be trained or experienced in short-term work.The service should have links with local mental health services and other agencies to enable referral where needed.

Traumatic incidents

Traumatic incidents may include physical or verbal assault, a drug error, involvement in a critical incident inquiry - for example, suicide or homicide - or witnessing a fatal accident. It is quite common for staff who have been exposed to traumatic incidents to develop a range of reactions and post-trauma symptoms, some of which may be distressing and disabling.Both in the short and longer term, the individual's well-being and performance may be severely affected.

Most symptoms generally diminish over a few weeks,but where they persist they may indicate the presence of Post Traumatic Stress Disorder (PTSD) or another psychological disorder.While only a small proportion of staff exposed to critical incidents develop PTSD, support following a traumatic incident at work should be available to all staff.Although this is a specialist area of work,which requires appropriate training, staff counselling services are in a good position to provide post incident support.

In addition,psychological debriefing should not be set up in isolation - the Department of Health's Treatment Choice in Psychological Therapies and Counselling states that it should only be employed where follow-up and access to other psychological support is available, for example, a staff counselling service.

Framework services

The way in which services are established is critical to their success. To ensure that services fulfil their potential, careful consideration of their purpose, structure and resourcing is required. Central to establishing a successful service is organisational ownership and the involvement of key stakeholders. A development or advisory group can help to ensure that the interests of the various stakeholders are taken into account. This should include senior management - for example the director of nursing or human resources - and the views of staff and unions, with their active involvement if possible, enabling users to have confidence in their service.

The broad aims of the service should be informed by human resource issues - like levels of stress and sickness absence, staff attitude surveys and critical incident records - but they must be realistic. For example, don't assume that establishing a counselling service will result in an immediate fall in sickness absence or reduce the threat of litigation.These can only be achieved if counselling is offered as part of a wider organisational response, specifically addressing the work factors that give rise to these concerns.

More achievable aims might include:

- providing timely psychological support to staff experiencing stress or distress, preventing further deterioration of symptoms and an adverse impact on work performance
- contributing to the return to work of staff whose psychological health has resulted in absence from work
- effectively managing critical incidents and providing appropriate support to staff affected.

The key objectives and functions of the service can be determined from the overall aims.Objective setting is important in that it provides the subsequent basis for evaluating the overall effectiveness of the service. Objectives will be specific to each organisation but should capture the contribution that services can make to staff as clients and to the wider organisation.Here are some examples:

— providing professional, short-term, confidential counselling to all staff

— providing counselling, both face-to-face and by telephone

— offering training and consultancy to managers to help staff who are experiencing distress

— providing post incident support to staff, including debriefing as appropriate

— contributing to organisational policy and practice in critical incident management.

Additional service objectives or functions may also be identified, for example:

— providing training for staff in counselling and communication skills,managing stress and psychological responses to traumatic situations

— offering mediation or conflict resolution . giving careers advice.

Both internal and external models of service delivery have their benefits and problems and a number of issues need to be considered before making a choice. These include the size of the organisation and whether it can sustain its own provision, or whether it would be better to contract with an external provider with an existing service. Geographical area may be a deciding factor and, if an external private provider is selected, you will need to ascertain whether it can provide what it claims.

However the service is provided, it should be based on a set of clear quality criteria that form the basis for monitoring and evaluating its quality and effectiveness. In terms of staff as clients, it can be important that they feel the counsellor understands the nature of their role within the organisation.Through its understanding of the organisation, the service can be highly responsive to need and also contribute to and inform the wider human resource agenda by, for example, advising on the management of major organisational change.

Clinical supervision of the work of counsellors is normally external and this is considered good practice in most workplace and other organisational settings.Provided the service is of a sufficient size, a service manager who is experienced in workplace counselling can be appointed to have responsibility for the clinical work of the service. The service needs to be located so as to protect the confidentiality of service users. Where the organisation covers a wide geographical area or is delivered from a range of different locations, thought should be given to ensuring that staff are able to access the service easily.

The appropriate level of resourcing for services will depend on a range of factors, including the size of the organisation, the anticipated uptake by staff, and the functions that the service is expected to provide. In UK, NHS Executive guidance suggests a ratio of one full-time counsellor per 2,000 staff, where counsellors have no role other than counselling, and where they work from a single site.More staff may be needed if the service fulfils additional functions or operates from different sites.

An alternative model for assessing the level of counselling resources required can be based on anticipated staff uptake and the optimum caseload capacity of counsellors. While usage cannot be predicted in advance, studies of workplace counselling provision suggest that an assumption that up to 10 per cent of staff may use the service in any one year is not unreasonable.

Broadly, there are two models within the health service—the first being NHS based workplace counselling services.These are located in one organisation, but also provide services to neighbouring trusts and other employers. This model tends to be the most popular amongst health service organisations without their own service. The second is the large number of commercial providers that offer a range of counselling and other services, usually known as Employee Assistance Programmes (EAPs). They mainly work off-site and their counsellors (sometimes called associates) are usually self-employed and may work for a number of EAP providers.

External provision may be appropriate for smaller organisations that cannot sustain their own internal provision, or where the organisation simply wants to provide counselling and nothing else.Larger EAPs cover a wide geographical area; offer 24-hour access to services and can provide a range of additional services, such as critical incident support and legal and debt advice.

NHS based providers will have a good understanding of the health service context and experience in delivering counselling to health service staff.Depending on how important this is to the purchasing organisation, this could form part of the specification. EAP providers may offer very comprehensive packages that the organisation does not require. One of the limitations of external provision is a lack of direct control over quality.

A clear system for reporting of service activity should be established at the outset.Reporting should enable the organisation to determine whether the service is achieving its aims and deal with any resource issues that may arise.The process should also seek to identify areas of concern that may need to be examined by the wider organisation, for example, a high proportion of service users experiencing bullying and harassment.

Counselling services and their role in wider staff support and organisational culture. Services that are purely reactive, only providing counselling for distressed employees, miss an important opportunity to help create a healthier organisation. For example, organisational change is now increasingly commonplace within the health service and is one area where staff counselling services can make a vital contribution.

Services routinely work with clients who are affected by victims of poorly managed change.They have a valuable role to play in discussions at management or board level about how proposed changes may impact operationally and the best way to implement them. Many organisations fail to recognise this contribution and need time to embrace this new way of working. If counselling services are provided internally, experience shows that most will need to be established for between two and three years before their role and functions are fully understood and they are able to contribute to the wider organisation.

There are a number of basic prerequisites for a successful integrated service. The organisation needs to recognise the potential contribution services can make to both individual staff and the wider organisation.The service needs to maintain its profile within the organisation and seek opportunities for contributing to the organisational agenda.

It requires counsellors who are comfortable about operating in an organisational context and can manage any tensions that may arise in meeting the needs of both the client and the organisation. Most counselling and staff support services within health service settings, particularly those that are more established and integrated, offer a range of additional services that contribute to a more comprehensive model of employee support,with overall staff well-being at their core.

Services have an important role to play in destigmatising issues of psychological distress.This may include educating others about coping with stress or understanding the psychological effects of trauma. Services can also provide training on issues like managing distressed staff, counselling skills and handling stress.This kind of educational activity provides opportunities for staff to meet counsellors in a different capacity, raising the profile of the service.

Providing confidential and objective career guidance through workplace counselling services can reap enormous benefits for both the individual and the organisation. Supporting staff to make career decisions helps to ensure a more motivated workforce and will ultimately increase retention rates. Services provided by career advisers include support with job applications and interview techniques, feedback on self awareness exercises and psychometric tests, guidance on educational and career options in the health service, support with personal development planning and access to a range of career resources.

Financial problems can impact on other aspects of life and, if not dealt with early, can have devastating results, even leading to the loss of a home. A preoccupation with financial difficulties can easily spill over into the work place and giving staff the opportunity to talk to an independent adviser, in confidence, can alleviate some of the stress and provide practical options for dealing with debt. At a minimum, services should have a list of resources for local debt advice, although in some areas arranging an appointment can take several weeks.

The counselling service should establish effective good links with the local statutory and voluntary sector mental health services to enable referral to alternative or additional sources of psychological or practical support. These may include other counselling and psychotherapy services, Citizens Advice Bureaux, law centres and and other agencies that offer support, such as GP practices and unions. Development of these links should be considered from the outset.

From an employer's perspective, the rationale for providing staff counselling is likely to be to improve psychological well-being, performance and attendance. All services should try to determine how effective counselling is in achieving these aims.Audit and evaluation should be integrated into service planning and development, ideally incorporating three key areas:

— routine audit of service utilisation

— routine audit of aspects of service quality, including effectiveness

— the overall objectives of the service.

Routine audit and evaluation are likely to inform the broader question of whether the service is meeting its overall objectives, helping to determine whether they remain realistic or need revision.Depending on the objectives of the service, some specific measures of effectiveness may be required. For example, if one of the service's objectives is helping staff suffering from stress to return to work,measures of pre and post counselling absence or work functioning will be required. Functions that are offered in addition to counselling may need their own individual evaluation frameworks.

The measurement of service utilisation, quality and effectiveness varies widely across psychological therapy services generally and workplace counselling is no exception.Most services routinely audit service utilisation and some seek client feedback on their experience of the service. A relatively small number have attempted to quantify the outcomes of counselling for their clients. Many of the measurement tools currently in use have been developed by individual services,with only a few appearing to use valid and reliable measures to evaluate effectiveness.

While these 'home grown' systems undoubtedly yield valuable data, their drawback is that they offer no opportunity for comparing data with other services and no possibility of determining whether the data is representative of the wider workplace counselling sector. The RCN's Counselling Service has been using a standardised system since March 1999. The CORE (Clinical Outcomes in Routine Evaluation) system is the first in the UK to apply audit, evaluation and outcome measurement to counselling and psychological therapy settings.

The RCN has been collaborating with the Psychological Therapies Research Centre and other partners to adapt CORE to the needs of workplace counselling, and has been part of a collaborative research project involving seven workplace counselling services using the CORE system. The findings of this research project build on the conclusions of the McLeod study that workplace counselling is highly effective. The study found that the psychological health profile of staff using counselling services is almost identical to that of clients using primary care counselling, and that workplace counselling has the potential to:

— improve mental health for 78 per cent of clients

— reduce rates of sickness and absence

— enhance work functioning.

Adolescents, who constitute over one-fifth of India's population, have limited access to vital information and services pertaining to sexual and reproductive health (SRH). Cultural taboos surrounding communication about sexual matters persist in the parent-child relationship, and young people have few opportunities outside their peer group to talk about their feelings and anxieties. Founded in 1949, the Family Planning Association of India (FPAI) is the country's largest nongovernmental organization (NGO) providing family planning and other reproductive health services.

In addition to clinical services, training and research, FPAI carries out extensive information, education and communications programmes throughout India. The FPAI has experimented with numerous programmes to meet the needs of both urban and rural youth, including campaigns to increase the age at marriage, sexuality and reproductive health education programmes, and counselling services.

In the late 1960s, FPAI began educating young people in schools, colleges and non-formal educational institutions on issues related to population and family life. These programmes provide an orientation for young people regarding sexuality, reproductive health, the prevention of unplanned pregnancies and sexually transmitted infections (STIs). In designing these programmes, the FPAI kept in view that adolescents have needs that are distinct from those of adults. These education programmes do not merely provide information, but also aim to enhance young people's communication skills, clarify values, change attitudes and prevent risky behaviour.

In 1978, FPAI established Sexuality Education Counselling Research Therapy/Training (SECRT) centres, which provide sexuality education and counselling. Today 37 SECRT centres have reached over 120 000 young people. SECRT centres offer counselling services to both married and unmarried adults and adolescents, on a range of topics, including premarital counselling, family planning, and marital and infertility counselling.

FPAI offers these services individually, in groups, by correspondence and over the telephone. FPAI has developed several innovative approaches in partnership with young people to promote sexual and reproductive health. The organization works through youth clubs in many settings to provide accurate information on family life and adolescent health matters, including the prevention of sexually transmitted infections, including human immmunodeficiency virus infection (STIs/HIV).

In addition, FPAI branches have developed peer educator initiatives in collaboration with other youth programmes, such as Youth Parliament, Young Women Information Centres and thespian programmes. In addition, FPAI has developed "Young Inspirers Clubs" in rural and urban areas. These clubs use folk media to raise awareness about STIs/HIV/AIDS, to eradicate myths and misconceptions related to sexuality, and to promote reproductive health.

In 1997, FPAI-SECRT initiated "Spearhead Youth Health Leadership Training Programme". This programme has trained nearly 1000 youth leaders, many of whom have served as peer counsellors in the FPAI Young Inspirers

Clubs. In 1999, the FPAI implemented a project on "Enhancing Sexual and Reproductive Health of Young Persons". This project aimed to extend information and counselling on issues related to human sexuality, preparation for marriage, responsible parenthood, gender issues, contraception and prevention of STIs/HIV/AIDS. As part of the project, the six FPAI branches carried out sensitization programmes, organized medical check-up camps and provided counselling and training for teachers and peer educators. The project reached out to rural and urban youth, and the response was overwhelming.

For example, the STI/HIV prevention programme reached 7065 young people, including 3391 out-of-school, illiterate youth. In Dharwad (Karnataka), the project established a strong network of young people trained to impart knowledge on sexuality and STIs/ HIV/AIDS. Its peer group leaders' training led to the establishment of eight community counselling centres in six villages where four to five peer group leaders provide counselling on a regular basis.

Psychological and Social Needs of Parents

"Support" is defined as including all activities or arrangements within the health care environment which help meet the psychological and social needs of parents whose children are receiving care, whether or not they are specifically intended to fulfil this purpose. Support thus covers a wide range of issues from practical arrangements for parents to stay in the hospital and help in their children's care to the giving of information, encouragement, advice and sympathy. It follows that anyone involved in the provision or organisation of care at an individual or institutional level may have a part to play in ensuring that parents' needs are provided for and taken into account. Support may also be provided from sources outside the health care setting including self-help groups or facilitator-led support groups.

Within the broader framework of psychological and social support, counselling is the activity which occurs when a person (either regularly or temporarily in the role of counsellor) offers time, attention and respect to another person or persons to explore their feelings and concerns. Counselling has been defined by Bor et al as:

> "An interaction in a therapeutic setting, focussing primarily on a conversation about relationships, beliefs and behaviour (including feelings), through which the patient's perceived problem is elucidated and framed or reframed in a fitting or useful way, and in which new solutions are generated and the problem takes on a new meaning."

There are four different levels of counselling in health care settings:

i *Information-giving*: the provision of factual information and advice about medical conditions, laboratory tests, treatments etc.

ii. *Implications counselling*: a discussion with the patient and/or others which addresses the implications of the information for the individual or family and their personal circumstances.

iii *Supportive counselling*: in which the emotional consequences of the information and its implications can be identified and addressed in a supportive and caring environment.

iv *Psychotherapeutic counselling*: focuses on healing, psychological adjustment, coping and problem resolution.

The first two levels are likely to be regarded as a routine part of care for all patients, which will usually be provided by the health professionals responsible for their medical and nursing care. In certain situations (such as bereavement and diagnostic testing for genetic disorders or HIV) where psychological issues are recognised as particularly significant, supportive counselling may also be offered to all patients. Formal psychotherapeutic counselling will not be needed by all patients and is more likely to be provided through referral to a specialist counsellor.

Counselling skills, such as listening, reflecting and conveying empathy, are not exclusive to the counsellor. Almost all health care professionals need such skills in the course of their interactions with patients, for example in giving information, clarifying treatment options and helping people adjust to new and sometimes unwelcome circumstances. The difference between these generic skills and those of a formally defined counsellor (or psychologist or psychotherapist) is that the latter is expected to have advanced training and qualifications in their field and is likely to approach the counselling process within a specific theoretical framework (such as humanistic counselling, psychodynamic counselling or cognitive behaviour counselling).

Families may present a number of times for therapy, each time with different needs and dilemmas with only minimal contact in between. Formal counselling interventions for families of children who are sick vary according to the task faced by the family. Examples include crisis counselling to help facilitate and contain emotional expression following diagnosis or relapse; insight-orientated psychotherapy for considering future uncertainty over illness; and family therapy when unacknowledged conflict, or differing opinion on appropriate coping strategies and communication, is resulting in problems such as non-compliance with therapies or refusing to eat.

Some of the problems experienced by parents are caused simply by being with their children in an unfamiliar institutional setting and are not specific to the hospital context or the child's illness or treatment. Other difficulties derive from the way in which hospitals in particular are organised and the role that parents are expected to play in their child's care. Others again reflect the inherent anxieties associated with serious illness and vary according to the circumstances of the individual child. Problems of being in a strange environment include:

— *lack of familiarity*: not knowing the way around, who is who, who does what, where and when to ask for information, how and when things happen, what to expect or what is expected of oneself

— *isolation*: from usual resources, social networks and one's own usual social roles

The ordinary care of any child involves meeting his or her physical, psychological, social and spiritual needs. These are normally met primarily by the family. Illness affects the nature of some or all of these needs, and also the ability of the family to meet them. Hospitalisation of a child forces changes in the parents' view of themselves as protectors and nurturers. They may have to relinquish much of their parenting role to the nurses, being anxious about performing even normal every day care on a sick child in an unfamiliar environment and not knowing what they are expected or permitted to do.

Parent's views about the amount of involvement they would like to have in their child's care vary and the same parents' views may change over time as their own and their child's circumstances alter. It is suggested that the best way of achieving an appropriate balance of care is through negotiation between nursing staff and individual families to reach agreement based on the parents' wishes rather than by imposing the expectations of the professional staff.

Participation is desired by parents and children and is also consistent with current discourse about empowerment and involvement of users in health care.Nevertheless, such involvement may exacerbate some of the financial, social and personal costs experienced by parents:

Financial costs may include: costs of travelling to hospital, especially where children are being treated in regional centres; extra costs of staying away from home (buying meals, telephones, paying for alternative care for siblings); loss of income (especially for those who are self-employed).

Social costs may include: using up holiday entitlement; depleting reserves of goodwill from employers, friends or neighbours who may be co-opted in to help

Personal costs Participation in unpleasant experiences (such as accompanying a child to the anaesthetic room, staying with them during a painful procedure or refusing to let them have a drink) has been identified as difficult because it challenges parents' ideas of themselves and their usual roles in providing for or protecting their children.This may be seen by parents and staff as something to be coped with, rather than avoided, because of the benefits to both child and parent of having the parent present and involved.

Suggested strategies for limiting some of the costs of parental involvement include:

— ensuring that parental costs are taken into account in the design of services (eg by ensuring parents are not expected to pay more than hospital workers for food and drink).

— enabling parents to choose whether or not to participate in their child's care and not to be required to be involved simply because of lack of nursing staff.

For all parents of children with serious illness, one of the most important sources of stress will be anxiety about the child itself and its condition. In a study of mothers whose children had been admitted unexpectedly to a paediatric intensive care unit, respondents described the sudden transition from having a healthy child to having a child who was critically ill as causing catastrophic feelings of shock, guilt, helplessness and confusion. Key issues identified included:

— the tension experienced while getting to and waiting for their partners to reach the hospital

— waiting in acute stress without nursing assessment or therapeutic support through a period of enforced separation during the medical stabilisation of the child obeing re-united with a child whose appearance had changed (being nursed naked, intubated, ventilated and attached to a variety of monitors and infusion devices)

A study of the experiences of parents whose children suffered neurological damage after cardiac surgery identified the following:

— shock, loss and grief, combined for some parents with a profound sense of "aloneness"

— guilt, blame and anger - almost all the parents identified a specific focus of blame for their child's brain damage. These included "medicine", "the driver", "the child" and "themselves"

— fear for their own sanity linked to emotional and physical exhaustion

— fear of injuring the disabled child and thoughts of euthanasia

The death of a child has been repeatedly identified as the most traumatic experience a family will endure. The grief process has been described as falling into three phases: a period of numbness, shock, disbelief and unreality; a period of intense grief; and a period of reorganisation and recovery. Additional feelings that may arise include anger, helplessness, rage, frustration and guilt. Behavioural reactions to these feelings can include hysteria, crying, wailing, hitting and physical acting out.Aspects of emotional support that have been found to be helpful to families after the death of a child in hospital include: listening, talking openly and honestly, providing words of comfort, showing feelings, providing privacy and choosing words carefully.

In a paediatric intensive care unit, families may be exposed to deaths of children other than their own. On such units, families often form their own support network and become important parts of each other's "family" while their children are ill. Witnessing the death of someone else's child in the unit will intensify fears of death and feelings of uncertainty about one's own child's outcome.

Watching a child die, especially if witnessed more than once, may also cast doubts on the belief that one's own child is receiving the best care possible. For all these reasons it is suggested that parents present during and after the death of a child other than their own have significant needs and their normal coping behaviours may be compromised if they feel their needs are insignificant compared with those of the bereaved family.

Waiting has been identified as one of the most stressful parts of the experience for parents of hospitalised children.Remaining inactive and unable to leave an area for fear of missing an important report denies an individual the mobility often used to deal with stress and can lead to feelings of powerlessness. Families who wait often feel neglected and forgotten. The expected event - a test result, a date for surgery or an improvement in the child's condition - is often unpredictable and uncertain. All of these characteristics may affect the parent's ability to cope with the stress of waiting.

Manifestations of waiting when the outcome is not known include fear, fatigue, anxiety, lack of ability to concentrate, restlessness, inability to eat or drink, anger and frustration. Stressful periods of waiting occur at various different stages in the child's care. These include waiting:

— for admission, for surgery and for discharge (all of which may be unexpectedly brought forward or postponed for a variety of reasons not always directly connected with the child involved)

— for the results of diagnostic tests (to know what is wrong and what the prognosis and required treatment may be)

— during surgery and medical treatment (waiting to know whether the child has come through alright and whether the treatment has been successful)

Some waiting is unavoidable (i.e. that related to the time it takes to perform tests, procedures and surgery and for a child's condition to improve) Other types of waiting could potentially be reduced or eliminated (that relating to admissions procedures, pain alleviation, delay in conveying medical reports and messages and arrival in a treatment area long before the procedure can be done). Following strategies to help parents cope with waiting include :

— acknowledge to parents that it is difficult to wait

— provide a comfortable setting in which to wait

— assist parents to find a support person to share the waiting

— be aware of parents' physical needs (for food etc) while they wait

— keep parents regularly informed of progress

— ensure a system for prompt delivery of messages

— assist parents to use coping strategies that have helped them before

— use hospital volunteers to maintain waiting areas and help meet parents' needs

— develop strategies for care delivery that minimise avoidable waiting

Parental Stress

Stress among parents of children admitted to paediatric intensive care units found that:

— parents experiencing unexpected admission of their child had higher stress scores on all dimensions than planned admission parents

— parents' overall stress levels are highest early on in the experience of hospitalisation and diminish over time (except where things go wrong)

— factors concerning the child (diagnosis, prognosis, experience of pain) and the parents' relationship with their child were major sources of stress and were more important to parents than factors affecting their own comfort, self-care or spiritual needs

Several studies have been undertaken to identify parents' own perceptions of their needs for support while their children are in hospital. Identified needs include:

— to receive accurate information about their child's condition that is honest, exact, understandable, ongoing, freely offered, consistent, well-timed and comprehensive

— to have ready access to their child, continue in the parental role, have meaningful participation in their care and be recognised as important to their recovery

— to trust in the staff and feel that they care about (as well as for) the child

— to be assured that the child is receiving the best care possible

— to receive support from their own social networks (including relatives, friends and workplace colleagues) and opportunities for the direct involvement of grandparents and siblings (include somewhere for the latter to play)

Needs identified by parents whose children who had suffered brain damage after surgery included:

— contact with other families in similar situations

— an individual with whom they could build a trusting one-to-one relationship (both at the time of the injury and afterwards) with the skills and detachment to discuss the tragedy openly and to listen to their doubts, anxieties or anger as parents. It was frequently suggested that this person should be detached from the child's care, available on a regular basis and easy to reach as required

— the provision of written summaries about their child's brain damage, to ease the burden of having to retell the story to every new contact

— information about local support services, within the first few weeks, repeated as required and in writing ofor the fate and future of children like their own to be openly discussed by society and by the medical profession.

The 1959 Platt Report on the welfare of children in hospital led to radical changes in, among other things, access and provision for parents. These original government recommendations were based on a psychological viewpoint, but research carried out subsequently added a sociological dimension based on the relationship between the child and family and the discontinuity in family life caused by hospital admission.Over the past few years there has been an increasing consensus between government, professional and voluntary organisations on the benefits of parental participation in "family-centred" care.

The 1991 guidance advises the agreement of service specifications which:

— recognise that parents and members of the immediate family are not visitors, encourage and assist them to be with their child at all times (especially those that are most stressful i.e. during anaesthesia, treatments, investigations and during post-operative recovery) and enable them to give continuous love, care, comfort and support to their child

— help parents to undertake many familiar tasks helpful to the care of their child and provide help and advice to continue the care following the child's discharge.

It also recommends that hospital routines should be sufficiently flexible to adapt to families' different cultural practices and that parents be encouraged to express their preferences for the care of their children in relation to diet and feeding, clothing, washing and bathing, and beliefs or traditions in respect of healing, treatment and care while dying

The 1991 guidance encourages health authorities and hospitals to establish links with voluntary organisations active in their areas to achieve maximum co-operation in the planning and organisation of services like social work support. It also recommends that those involved in agreeing contracts should ensure that:

— all staff are sensitive to the needs of children and their families with life-threatening conditions and are able to draw upon staff specifically trained in care and counselling

— parents are informed in an appropriate manner, as soon as possible of their child's condition and given every opportunity to talk through their feelings

— care is taken not to "avoid" parents whose child is dying, while at the same time recognising the need for privacy

— where children are taken home, advice is available to parents on the help available from statutory or voluntary agencies to ensure ongoing support and counselling for as long as necessary oparents have the opportunity to return to the hospital to find out anything further they wish to know about any aspect of their child's illness, care or treatment

When a child dies, the 1991 guidance states that it is essential that parents/carers are helped to cope with the sense of loss and grief and also given practical assistance to help them make necessary decisions. Health authorities and hospitals are advised to ensure that:

— a member of staff trained in care and counselling is designated to give families, including siblings, all the necessary support including help with the arrangement of bereavement counselling and practical issues like burial arrangements

— the results of any post mortem investigation are conveyed in a sympathetic manner to the family in order that the therapeutic value of the discussion of the pathologist's findings is fully realised.

— the family's GP is informed as soon as possible so that, as necessary, the GP can help them cope with the medical effects of bereavement

The 1996 Children's Charter contains a number of statements about the rights and expectations of parents whose children are sick. These include rights:

— to take part in any discussions and decisions about the child's treatment and care and to be kept up to date with their progress

— for the child to have a named consultant paediatrician or surgeon and named qualified nurse to look after them and provide quality of care

— to stay in hospital with the child, participate in their care, accompany them to the anaesthetic room and be informed about pain relief

In addition to the Department of Health guidance, a number of professional and voluntary bodies have made recommendations in recent years concerning the care of children in hospital . Most of these endorse or reiterate the standards contained in the DoH guidance in relation to parental involvement and support. Some go into more detail about how services should be managed in this respect or make additional recommendations.

A 1995 report by the British Paediatric Association (BPA) points up the "vital role" of the specialist social worker. It observes that the combination of social work skills and knowledge of rare and life threatening conditions give them an advantage in dealing with the problems that arise in families when a child has a serious disease or organ failure. It observes that in some regions, specialist social worker posts have been reduced or discontinued because of new funding arrangements. Guidance relating to parent's needs included recommendations for: information:

— about wards and hospital facilities on admission

— about the reasons for starvation before operations and on what the child can eat and drink and when

— about the illness and the operation, preparation for the operation, operating procedures and routines, how to help the child, aftercare, where and how to obtain further information and advice.

— about where parents can wait during the operation, how long the child is likely to be and about what is happening if delays occur

— about what to expect in the recovery room and their role

— about the likely condition of their child after the operation

— about the outcome of the operation or procedure at the earliest opportunity by a member of the surgical team and reinforced by the recovery room and ward nurses

— on how to care for the child after discharge and an emergency number to contact

— an agreed policy on the information to be given to parents on the ward and a checklist to avoid duplication or conflicting information

— a policy and procedure for interpreting services for families who do not speak

In 1988, a working party involving the British Paediatric Association, the King's Fund and the National Association of Health Authorities produced guidelines on the care of dying children and their families.These go into considerable detail into the support needs of parents at all stages from diagnosis to bereavement including, for example, the need to:

— ensure that parents are centrally involved and treated with respect as partners in the care

— ensure good communication between parents and professionals

— ensure that parents have adequate finance

— ensure that parents are aware of the range of people (and self-help groups), both in hospital and in the community, who might help by listening and talking

— give parents the opportunity to talk to other parents in a similar situation

— offer continuity, friendship and sensitive support, responding to individual needs.

Counselling Programmes for Men

Violence against women in relationships is physical or sexual assault or threat of assault. Violence may occur within ongoing or "separated" relationships, regardless of marital status. Other behaviours such as intimidation, stalking, psychological abuse, sexual abuse, financial exploitation and spiritual abuse should be recognized as part of the continuum of power and control that men use against young and elderly women alike. The following are the some examples in each of these categories:

1. Physical assault includes grabbing, restraining, slapping, punching, shoving, choking, biting, kicking, shaking, burning with a cigarette, throwing hot liquids, tying up, using weapons (knives, guns, sticks and other objects). Physical abuse also includes the removal of basic necessities (e.g. medications, health care, crutches, food, sleep) and forced alcohol or drug use.

2. Psychological abuse includes expressions of excessive jealousy, mistrust, control, threats, verbal abuse and destruction of property. Examples of controlling behaviours include forbidding a woman to go to school, learn English or have a driver's licence. Men who are psychologically abusive may try to limit whom their partners visit or talk to on the phone, so that the women become isolated from friends and relatives. They may even harass the women at work with repeated phone calls and visits. Examples of threatening behaviours include threatening to use violence against her or her children, to take away the children, to have her deported, to commit suicide if she does not comply with his demands or to have her institutionalized. Non-verbal forms of psychological abuse may include glaring, fist shaking, physical intimidation and hitting doors or walls. Verbal abuse consists of yelling, degrading comments, put-downs, blaming and unfounded accusations about her loyalty or sexual behaviour. It is important to remember that, although a woman who experiences frequent psychological abuse often lives with ongoing fear of her partner, she may never have been the victim of an act that could have brought the man before the courts.

3. Sexual abuse and sexual assault are non-consensual, violent acts that compromise the sexual integrity of the victim. These acts include rape, demands for sex in a way that degrades the victim, use of penetrating objects and any form of physical abuse directed at the sexual areas of the body or done during sexual activity. Sexual abuse can also include deliberate infection with HIV or with other sexually transmitted diseases (either refusal to use a condom or failure to

reveal the possibility of infection), forcing her to prostitute herself, refusing to take "no" for an answer, initiating sex after violence.

4. Financial abuse includes denying a woman access to or knowledge of the family's money, preventing her input regarding purchases, forbidding her to have a bank account, denying access to her own money, not paying child support, not allowing her to work or launching legal actions so as to deplete her economic resources.
5. Spiritual abuse occurs when a woman's spiritual beliefs are ridiculed or attacked or when she is prevented from attending the religious services of her choice. The man may demand that she attend his religious gatherings or pray in the manner that he dictates. Her children may be raised in a different faith or tradition against her will.

There are a variety of theories explaining men's violence toward their partners. The following are five of the major approaches to understanding men's violence in relationships. Many counsellors and programs are influenced by more than one of the following views:

Psycho-dynamic/Insight Theory

Early theories as to the cause of men's violence against women emphasized psychological problems related to childhood trauma, developmental difficulties or mental illness. Problems include immature personalities, personality disorders, poor impulse control, fear of intimacy and/or abandonment and psychiatric illnesses. Some counsellors express concern that attributing men's violence to individual pathology tends to remove responsibility for the behaviour from the perpetrator and place it in the hands of a professional who is to provide treatment.

Dr. Anne Ganley, a pioneer in the field, indicates that she did not find a higher proportion of mental illness among men who assault their partners than among men who did not. However, she did provide a separate counselling group for men who suffered either from a mental illness requiring medication or had some form of organic brain syndrome. This approach is based on the view that once the organic problem is managed through medication, the man can learn to take responsibility for his abusive behaviour and learn respectful ways of communicating.

Sonkin indicates that for some men, individual therapy can provide an awareness of powerful unconscious emotions, an important first step in taking control of their violence. The danger is that awareness may not necessarily translate into a cessation of violence and the use of power and control at home. If these actions continue to go unchallenged by the criminal justice system, a man's sense of power over her may increase. Other critics of this approach argue that it may not deal with immediate safety issues and ignores the control that the violent behaviour exerts over the victim. Responsible individual counselling focuses on safety concerns first, then explores attitudes that condone violence against women, and finally examines childhood trauma issues.

Ventilation Theory

Although used infrequently as an intervention with assaultive men, the risks associated with this approach warrant mentioning here. Research does not support this theory's main assumption that the ventilation of anger will result in less anger and stress. Tavris reported that venting anger can become addictive to the user. Straus found that verbal aggression is strongly associated with increases in physical aggression. Ganley expressed concern that when assaultive men release their anger using a punching bag or chopping wood, it can result in reinforcing the behaviour through repetition. In addition, it provides the message that the only way to deal with anger or conflict is through a physical explosion. Ventilating anger suggests that violence is only an anger management problem. This ignores the fact that many men are just as angry in other situations in which they are not violent or controlling.

Family Systems Theory

Usually implemented through couple's therapy, family systems theory (FST) views both victim and perpetrator as participating in maladaptive ways of interacting. Violence serves a function of maintaining distance or reinforcing certain family dynamics already in place. Many feminists voice concern that FST undercuts the seriousness of violence by taking the responsibility for the violence out of the hands of the perpetrator. In addition, FST may ignore the power differences between men and women in our society. Viewing the cause of violence as systemic may indirectly reinforce the view that the woman is responsible for her husband's feelings and actions. Real communication is not possible as long as violence, or the threat of violence, continues.

Cognitive-behavioural and Psycho-educational Theories

These approaches make the violence in the relationship the primary focus of intervention. Because violence is considered to be a learned behaviour, non-violence can be learned as an alternative. The techniques used in a psycho-educational approach include "anger logs" to separate thoughts, feelings and behaviours; time-outs to stop aggressive behaviour; stress management techniques; the identification of dysfunctional thinking that escalates anger; and interpersonal skills training such as communication and assertiveness techniques.

This model has been criticized for "taking too narrow a view of men's abusive behaviour and not addressing the function of this behaviour in maintaining power and control over women by individual men and by men as a class".

Pro-feminist Theory

Men's violence is a way to maintain power and control over women. The ways men oppress women through the use of violence include rape, physical aggression and threats. Violence, according to this theory, includes psychological abuse that can undermine the self-esteem of the victim. Two principles have been identified, fundamental to a feminist view of violence against women: "(1) No woman deserves to be beaten, and (2) men are solely responsible for their actions".

The profeminist model supports teaching anger management and communication skills but stresses the need to challenge men's sense of entitlement regarding women and children. Without a challenge to the power imbalance between men and their families, new skills can be misused by men as more sophisticated means to maintain control. From this perspective, work with assaultive men must seek to change social, legal and economic systems that support the oppression of women. Critics of the feminist approach suggest that it ignores individual personality issues that contribute to violence.

In Canada, there is a strong trend toward the use of a psycho-educational model, based on a feminist analysis of men's use of power. Many counsellors are influenced by the work of Alan Jenkins, which assumes that men will change more quickly when they are respected as individuals. In the context of a respectful relationship with a counsellor, a man can be challenged to face the violent and controlling behaviours that, in the long run, are damaging to him as well.

Counselling for assaultive men is just one strategy being promoted in support of the goal of ending violence against women and children. Counselling programs are frequently situated within the community as one part of an overall community intervention approach to ending violence in families. The groundbreaking work of the Duluth Domestic Abuse Intervention Project promotes this type of integrative approach. It stresses the use of a coordinated community response involving the cooperation of the criminal justice system, women's shelters and counselling agencies, assaultive men's intervention programs, and other community members and agencies concerned with ending violence against women in relationships.

Community work may include intervention to stop or prevent child abuse, workshops for students of all ages about non-violent approaches to conflict resolution, and campaigns to educate the public about the frequency and severity of violence against women in relationships.

Alcohol does not cause violence, although it may intensify its nature. A belief in male privilege over women forms the foundation for violent and controlling behaviours. Being drunk or on drugs provides an excuse for many men who say, "I'm only violent when I'm high so I'm not really a violent person." Although some men are only physically violent when drinking, their use of other forms of power and control generally continues or may escalate when they stop drinking.

A man who has a problem with alcohol or drug abuse and has been violent, even once, may have two separate problems: one with substance abuse and a second with violence and controlling behaviours. When the immediate threat of violence is removed or reduced through criminal charges, separation, incarceration or other means, it is important that the man begin substance abuse counselling first. If he begins an intervention program for his violence before substance abuse counselling, he is at risk of resorting to drugs or alcohol as an escape from the stress of confronting his abusive behaviour.

A residential treatment centre can provide intensive treatment of his substance abuse and, as a by-product, significantly reduce the risk to his family members. Chemically dependent, assaultive men may enter a substance abuse program assuming that it will also end their violence. In many cases, these men will continue to be abusive even after successfully completing such a program if they do not confront their use of violence and control in relationships.

Research shows that men who drink regularly are more likely to abuse family members. For example, one study shows that fathers who drank to excess were six times as likely to use violence against their own children compared to those who were not heavy drinkers. This study shows that the rates of wife assault for women living with men who drink regularly is triple the rate of those women whose partners do not drink at all. Canadian , National Violence Against Women Survey indicates that in one half of all violent partnerships, the perpetrator was drinking before an assault. Women whose partners frequently consumed five or more drinks at one time were at six times the risk of violence compared to those whose partners never drank.

The victim may also have a substance abuse problem. Although this may have pre-dated the violent relationship, it may be linked to the man's violence and abuse. He may pressure his partner to drink or use drugs or she may use drugs or alcohol as a means to numb the physical and emotional pain she experiences as a result of ongoing abuse. Women in these situations are especially vulnerable to abusing prescription drugs. She may receive these from a physician who is treating her for depression or anxiety caused by the violence she is experiencing at home. If she is abusing drugs or alcohol, it may leave her more vulnerable to his violence by compromising her ability to assess danger for herself and her children.

Furthermore, some women prefer to believe that their partner is not violent but only has a drinking problem. It may be hard to face the fact that the man she loves, or at one time did love, is abusive. She will need information and support to help identify other forms of power and control that he may be using when he is not under the influence of alcohol.

Marriage Counselling

Marriage or relationship counselling is based on the assumption that each person feels safe to say what she or he thinks and feels. There are documented cases of couples in marital therapy in which the man threatened or assaulted the woman after a session for saying something that he wanted kept secret, often his violence against her. If either party feels coerced into attending marital therapy, the person should consider individual counselling. When a therapist hears of, or suspects, violence in the relationship, it is important to assess the level of risk by speaking with each partner separately.

If there continues to be a risk of violence and controlling behaviours, the perpetrator should be referred to group or individual counselling focused on dealing with these issues before relationship counselling continues. Some counsellors place value on keeping the marriage together over the well-being of the individuals in the marriage. The therapist and the husband might imply that, "for the sake of the children," the woman should remain with her husband. Research shows that staying together "for the sake of the children" can be more detrimental than divorce if there is a significant degree of conflict between the parents.

Amato and Keith reviewed a large number of studies examining the effects of divorce on children. Higher rates of problems were evident among children whose parents were in more conflict, whether the couple was still together or divorced, than among children of parents in less conflict.

In some regions of Canada, there are programs for children who are exposed to abuse. Even if a specialized program does not exist, a skilled child therapist can help children cope with feelings related to the abuse and help them realize that they are not to blame. In some provinces, exposure to violence in the home is included in child welfare legislation. In responding to the needs of a family in which woman abuse has occurred, it is important to keep in mind the needs of the children for safety and security.

When professionals suspect child abuse, they have a legal duty to report to child protection authorities. The father's access may have to be restricted or supervised in situations where children have witnessed violence or been the victims of abuse. Professionals should be aware that children may need support and/or counselling after these visits. The woman may need extensive support, both legal and emotional, to resist allowing the father contact with the children when it is not in their best interest.

Several provinces now have a professional association of counsellors who work with assaultive men. These associations also have, in many cases, formal standards of practice. To help you identify some basic issues, obtain a copy of the standards from the association in your province or territory. These associations often maintain lists of member counsellors of programs who subscribe to the standards of practice.

Men who are violent and abusive in their relationships have the same variety of problems that non-violent men do. Some men will benefit from individual therapy as well as group therapy. Before embarking on counselling for their assaultive behaviour, some men will require substance abuse counselling first. During group counselling, traumatic childhood issues may arise and the men may require individual counselling as well. Men who suffer from a mental illness will require psychiatric assessment and treatment for the mental illness, in addition to group counselling for violence. When the abusive and controlling behaviour has stopped and the woman feels safe, the two may wish to participate in relationship counselling.

Men who are veterans or immigrants from war-torn countries may need additional help with issues related to torture or other experiences that may have produced post-traumatic stress disorder. Responsible programs screen out men who are not likely to benefit. Criteria for exclusion may include the following: active and untreated substance abuse problems, severe mental illness, high lethality, extreme denial, and brain injury. Entering a group therapy program can increase risk in some cases, as some men meet any challenge with violence or intimidation.

Counselling programs should not be a substitute for jail. Men who have spent some time in jail for assaulting their partner often report that the experience of going to jail helped them stop and think twice about using violence again. Although anger management skills are taught in most counselling programs, they are not the same. Anger management can be described as focusing on "three main areas:

(1) stress management and relaxation training,

(2) identification of emotions and cognitive restructuring, and

(3) interpersonal skills development".

Anger management can help a man to stop his violence and recognize that he can control his anger and be responsible for his behaviour. However, counselling that focuses mainly on anger management misses the point that violence may only be resorted to by a man when other techniques to maintain control over his partner have not been effective. Furthermore, many men feel just as angry with others in their lives but do not "lose control" and become violent. It is important for counselling programs to assist men in confronting the attitudes about women that make her feelings, needs and ideas less important than his.

Some ethnic communities run their own programs that address culturally specific conditions contributing to violence and allow men to express themselves in their own language. These programs should be accessed whenever possible. Programs for specific ethnic communities will address the same core issues as programs for the dominant culture, but will present these in culturally sensitive ways.

When men of visible and ethnic minorities enter mainstream programs for assaultive men, it is important that counsellors are aware of the impact that immigration, extended family issues and differing beliefs, attitudes and values have upon these clients.

The man's counsellor or another staff person from his program should be in touch with the partner of an abusive man. Initially, the practitioner will want to talk to her about the relationship and the history and nature of the violence and abuse. At this time, she should be given information about formulating a safety plan, if she does not already have one. She should be referred to counselling, support, and legal services for herself and her children. Periodically, she should be contacted to ascertain whether there has been any recurrence of violence or threats.

Without this type of follow-up, there is no mechanism by which to gauge the effectiveness of the program. Every woman should know that she has a right to her privacy and may, at any time, refuse to respond to requests of information by the program. If she chooses, the woman may be apprised of her partner's attendance, the length and content of the program, but not the details of the discussions that take place during her partner's counselling. Some communities will not have programs for assaultive men but will have counsellors who provide standard counselling services only to individuals. The woman has the right to expect the above basic information from any counsellor.

Counselling is not an "instant fix." However, his use of physical violence and threats should stop immediately. If not, the degree of his commitment to change may be questionable. A woman should anticipate that he will begin to remove himself from the home or take "time-outs" when he starts to get angry, and that he will stop other abusive, intimidating and controlling behaviours. In time, he should be able to listen to her concerns and demonstrate respect for her as an individual with needs and wants which are different from his own.

Women should be cautioned that some men may stop violent or threatening behaviours that could have legal consequences but escalate other controlling or manipulative tactics to maintain a position of domination in the relationship. A man's attending counselling is not a guarantee that he will stop his use of violence and controlling behaviours. Underneath a thin veneer of normalcy, women who have been victims of violence often feel isolated, confused and powerless, and suffer from low self-esteem.

Supportive counselling by a woman-centred agency or counsellor experienced in working with assaulted women can help the victim understand that the violence is not her fault. It can help her decide how she can take steps to protect herself and her children and what legal means are available to her. Because a man has completed a counselling program, it does not mean that she "owes" him reconciliation. Pressures to reunite, in the form of promises to change, gifts and tears, threats over child custody or support, and demands to accept his apology, are examples of his continued abuse and attempts to exert control over her life.

Even though there are groups for assaultive men in every major Canadian city and in many rural areas, not all men can or will change their violent and abusive behaviour. A woman may want the counsellor to tell her if her partner is safe to live with again, yet she is really the best judge of her own safety. Some men make good use of a group program and can become respectful and caring partners. Others may appear to learn and participate in the group, but maintain a domineering approach to their partner and children in the home.

Even if the counselling appears to have helped the man, it is still important to provide the woman with support and information about a safety plan, legal means and where to go for counselling for herself and her children. When women are violent toward their partners, it is often self-defence. In some cases, the woman is the one to initiate and sustain the violence. Although there is an ongoing debate over the extent to which women use violence in relationships, many more women are seriously harmed and killed by their spouse than are men.

In British Columbia, the Policy on Violence Against Women in Relationships is intended to cover "vulnerable males" as well as the assault of women. Men commonly minimize the frequency and severity of violence and abuse. Women may do so as well, unable to acknowledge the frequency and severity of the abuse they live with, or in response to his demands to keep it a secret. It is important to realize that physical violence is just one form of power and control and that financial abuse, psychological abuse, intimidation, isolation, sexual pressure and sexual assault can have an equally damaging impact on the victim. For these reasons, even a man who has truly used physical violence for the first time should receive counselling that focuses on his use of power and control in his relationship.

Individual Psychotherapy

Individual psychotherapy can help an assaultive man explore issues from his past, examine attitudes that contribute to his domination of women, and learn skills to establish healthy relationships. However, group therapy with other men who share the same problems can reduce isolation, denial and minimization and provide a positive experience of real peer support. Men who are hostile and resistant to the idea of going to a group for "wife-beaters" will often open up more quickly and begin to take responsibility for their actions when they interact with a group of men who have similar problems.

By attending group counselling, men can learn different ways of relating to other men, including honestly discussing feelings and issues and showing respect when discussing women, rather than stereotyping them. In communities where appropriate group therapy for assaultive men is not available, individual therapy with a professional with the appropriate knowledge and skill is the next best alternative. The majority of programs run from three to six months. Just because a man has completed a program of any length is no guarantee that he is safe and respectful in his relationships with women.

For this reason, several programs have a policy of expelling men who either do not participate or actively maintain a closed and hostile attitude. No number of sessions will help change a man who continues to blame his partner and/or the criminal justice system for his behaviour or who refuses to make a commitment to change. When a man realizes that improving his ways of relating to everyone in his life is a life-long process, he is on his way.

5

Psychodynamic Career Counselling

Counselling was transforming from the perspective of individual psychology to a perspective, which was social and dialectical. Counselling was crystallizing around the notion that counselling should be a process which helped people become eligible to participate (more fully or more competently) in daily sociocultural life. With this perspective counsellors and psychologists had been socialized into was that counselling was a procedure for "changing behavior" and for changing what goes wrong in the heads of people.

Neither the individualistic nor the environmental theorists and practitioners had seriously considered the interactive nature of human social life. Counselling is not so much a psychological method as it is a social practice or cultural method. In other words, counselling should be based on cultural hypotheses and principles and should not be presented as a "quasi-scientific" model based either individualistic psychology or environmental conditioning.

A culture-based counselling process that was construed as a social practice would reduce counsellor-other alienation. Further, such a move should make counsellor-other cooperation and joint-action much more feasible and meaningful. The notion that counselling should be moved from a psychological base to a multi-disciplinary or social base, and from scientific pretensions to cultural knowledge was too drastic and revisionary for most colleagues.

In many academic settings, there was, and continues to be, a rather cozy marriage between counselling and psychotherapy. Both are based on various psychological theories of personality development, deviation, and individual adjustment and both continue to borrow rather heavily from the medical model of curing people. Instead they need to make and/or use culturally sensible ideas and actions which will enable them to navigate and participate in everyday social life.

Most people asking for counselling help want to learn how to perform more successfully in everyday living. Often, they are trying to find, or make, their own compass of meaning that will give purpose to their daily actions. Finally, many help-seekers are seeking opportunities for "giving voice" to their life stories, issues that concern them, dilemmas that they face. They do not present behaviors to be changed as much as they present stories of human struggle for meaning and a desire to participate more rewardingly in socio-cultural life.

Many help-seekers are seeking situations which afford them the opportunity to voice "who" they are and want to be; and to tell how they are experiencing life in their particular social space. In North American counselling, spirituality was virtually a forbidden territory, even though for some help-seekers this was the most important part of their lives. Spiritual issues were considered as "nonscientific" or "too personal", or "mine-fields of prejudice and bias."

By the late 1980s the counselling perspective which would minimize or eliminate some the features of conventional counselling approaches which no longer believed to be sensible or tenable. Language is a good example. Language exists prior to the birth of the person. Following birth, through interaction with parents and others, the growing-up begins to appropriate language. It is best to think of language as a system of cultural tools. Bit by bit the tools of language move from the social interaction surrounding and engaging the child to the consciousness of the child. What was first in the parent and in the child-parent interaction becomes a working tool internally for the child. The flow of language and the use of language are both part of our socio-cultural "situation" and at the same time a set of tools which the individual employs to interact with others in a meaningful and competent way.

In other words, language in the form of utterances, words, symbols, metaphors, maps, drawings, and texts are cultural tools - or social mediators of experience. In 1988 a research project to investigate how counselling should be revised and what revisions would be most preferred in order to make counselling resonant with postmodern, post-industrial society. This project covered a period of five years and produced a framework for a new form of counselling, which initially had the title, "Constructivist career counselling".

Subsequently this "new look" in counselling was named SocioDynamic Counselling. Since it was developed as a holistic counselling perspective that unified five sectors of self and social life, the qualifier "career" was dropped as redundant. The sectors of self and social life to which the SocioDynamic perspective applies are:

1. learning/worklife
2. personal/relational life
3. spirituality
4. health/body
5. creativity/recreational.

Three assumptions of the new counselling perspective are:

— *Assumption No. 1:* Counselling as a discipline and as a practice should be moved from a positivist base to a constructivist base. This implies a different perspective on what knowledge is, on how we get knowledge, and on how knowledge is used in the practice of everyday life.

  a. *Ontology-acceptance of the principle of multiple realities:* This means that local, particular, constructed realities must not be supplanted by probabilistic, generalized knowledge as advocated by positivism. This stance legitimizes cultural variations, gender differences, life space differences, and places many practical truth claims in the domain of cultural sensibility rather than scientific proof.

  b. *Epistemology-shifting from a dualist/objectivist belief to a participatory, created knowledge belief:* We do not observe reality from an objective, detached position; we create realities through participation in whatever it is that we choose to call reality. As counsellors, we do not know from an objectivist, expert stance; we do know from a culturally participative activity.

c. *Methodology-shifting from scientific hypotheses and quantitative, rational analysis to sociocultural study methods of analysis:* This implies that counsellors in their practice should adopt a phenomenological, dialogical, hermeneutic stance for describing the particulars of the counselling process and relationship, and for describing the life space of the other.

— *Assumption No. 2:* Counselling should be situated in the context of post-modernity. This means a shift in emphasis from an intellectual position which favors the accumulation of authoritative knowledge and generalization to a focus on complexity, interrelationships, uniqueness, invention, and local knowledge. A post-modern stance means giving up meta-narratives such as beliefs in the primacy of science as the only legitimate route to knowledge, the certainty of "progress", and foundational thinking in general.

— *Assumption No. 3:* Counselling should be made sensible within the context of social life. This means adjusting to the requirements of a de-traditionalizing world taking into account the post-industrial elements of increased intercultural mixing, the transitional nature of working life, the increasing speed and unpredictability of socioeconomic change and the globalization of communication and economic systems. It also means revising ways of thinking about categories essential to counselling such as the self, relation, and meaning.

Our tools for construction of distinctly human patterns of living are human utterances, sentences, words, and symbols. Human languages are themselves human creations. In counselling as in living, generally we are dealing with linguistic descriptions of the world, our cultures and institutions, our relations, ourselves. While there is a natural world "out there", what we as humans mainly live by and with is linguistic descriptions. Descriptions are not "out there." They are human creations and interpretations. The "world out there" does not speak. Only we do. The human self is created by the use of vocabulary. Languages are made, not found. Selves, in the sense of symbolic meaning, are made, and do not exist as essences, waiting to be found, diagnosed, or measured.

The appeal of this new vocabulary may promote the search for new forms of nonlinguistic action and behavior thus leading to new forms of counselling practice, new ways of being a counsellor and new ways of making meaningful paths in culture. In this way counselling as a humanly created praxis for helping others has a chance to evolve intelligently in the context of new and changing conditions of intellectual and social life. The SocioDynamic perspective does not encourage doing the same old things in the same old ways. It suggests that if we stop doing those things, and try doing something else, we may be constructively surprised, amazed, and inspired at the results.

Of course many people try desperately, and insist that others settle on certainties and truths and then live accordingly. Increasingly, this certainty-based perspective is not tenable in postmodern social life. Instead we are more likely to make sense with those we help, and to ourselves, if we see our ideas as provisional, under development, as being dynamic and non-linear. This makes for an improvisational approach to human action, and to counselling, but it allows counsellors to remain close to the particulars of any sociocultural situation and to the ongoing life-experience of people. The SocioDynamic perspective does not offer arguments against the other counselling vocabularies that it wishes to replace with a new vocabulary.

Counselling, similar to therapy, is often discussed as a "talking cure" or "merely words and feelings." Introducing the concept of counselling skill as the use of cultural tools is a big step in the direction of materialization. The production of texts, transcripts, recordings, videos and the creation of maps in the counselling process are all rather obvious examples of materialization. Cultural tools by themselves cannot do anything. They only take on function when agents use them. Agents without cultural tools cannot perform in significant ways either. For meaningful action to occur, agents require tools and tools require agents. A life space map, for example, is an excellent example of a cultural tool (the map) which exists in time and space beyond the moments of its creation, thus allowing for its characterization as a socially created artifact (material object).

The use of material objects as cultural tool results in changes in agents. As counsellors we should be concerned with the development in others of skills in using cultural tools. The development of such skill requires acting with, and reacting to, the material properties of tools. Without material properties, there is nothing to act with, or react to, hence we have the phenomenon of counselling as "just talk" which soon vanishes with little or no trace when the conversation is ended. SocioDynamic Counselling may be best described as a language game in which metaphors are used for: "this is what happens", "this is how it happens", and "this is how people feel influenced by what is going on."

It is a language game in which social artifacts are produced in the form of maps, signs, diagrams, charts, icons, drawings, letters, recordings, videos, journal entries, collages, inscribed metaphors, and written scenarios and characterizations. These artifacts become cultural tools for the purpose of identifying mental appropriations, especially meanings. SocioDynamic Counselling is not grounded in theories of personality, motivation, or behavior. Since 1994, there were organize and implement a number of projects which have furthered the materialization of SocioDynamic Counselling:

1. Writing a counsellors' book: SocioDynamic Counselling
2. Writing Trainer Guidebook for Constructivist Counsellor Training
3. Co-sponsoring the Project for At Risk Youth using SocioDynamic Counselling in Toronto, under the auspices of the Toronto School Board
4. Providing training for counsellors in Denmark.
5. Providing training for counsellors in Finland
6. Providing training for Swedish counsellors
7. Intitiating a cooperative project with George Brown College in Toronto in offering a certificate program in Constructivist Career Counselling
8. Developing and implementing a constructivist peer career counselling training program for the Canadian Steel Trades Employees Commission in Toronto This

project was concluded in 1996 after a group of 30 counsellors had received training. Over a five year period about 6,000 unemployed steelworkers received group and or individual counselling for worklife planning

9. Instituting a Mentoring Project for career counsellors in the Public Service Commission of the Yukon Territorial Government assisting to implement constructivist career counselling in the worker re-integration project

These nine projects constitute a strategy materializing SocioDynamic Counselling.

Policies for Career Guidance and Counselling

The awareness of the value of good information and guidance for effective career, learning and labour market planning and decision making purposes is reflected in the description and rationale for the British Columbia (BC) New Directions in LMI initiative... "In today's world, efficient and timely collection, processing, analysis and application of information is viewed as an essential requirement for effective planning and decision making. This is particularly true in the case of career, learning and labour market information, where both individuals and organizations are making human capital investment decisions based on current and future trends and developments in the labour market."

The term "information, guidance and counselling services" (IGCS) refers to services intended to assist individuals, of any age and at any point throughout their lives, to make educational, training and occupational choices and to manage their careers. It includes a wide range of activities. For example activities within schools to help students clarify career goals and understand the world of work; personal or group-based assistance with decisions about initial courses of study, courses of vocational training, further education and training, initial job choice, job change, or work force reentry; computer-based or on-line services to provide information about jobs and careers or to help individuals make career choices; and services to produce and disseminate information about jobs, courses of study and vocational training. It includes services provided to those who have not yet entered the labour force, services to job seekers, and services to those who are employed.

Information Guidance and Counselling Services (IGCS) in British Columbia are highly decentralized. Delivery and management is at the community level, through contracted services, educational institutions or locally based government offices. The authority for directing these activities is distributed across a variety of ministries and agencies. While characterized by minimal formal authority, IGCS are nonetheless seen as an important component of, or contributor, to the success of a number of Provincial Ministries.

These Ministries have an interest in the delivery and success of IGCS as they support their legislated goals and objective. One example of this importance given to IGCS is the inclusion of Career and Personal Planning in the curriculum requirements for graduation from BC secondary schools. In addition to the government ministries and agencies there are a significant number of non-government stakeholders who are active in the development, management and delivery of IGCS. These stakeholders, or the members of their organizations, have primary responsibility for the delivery of IGCS to students or targeted clients.

Information, Guidance and Counselling materials that provide outcome information on public and private training programs have been developed to assist with career decision making, and to document the outcomes of programming. Over the last few years the roles of colleges have been evolving and hybrid university colleges have been introduced in BC. University colleges are able to provide a broader range of academic courses and to grant degrees.

While this is a cost effective alternative to sending students off to Vancouver or Victoria for education, there is a concern that trades and vocational programming, which are more technical and costly to provide, will become less accessible. At universities, the staff of career, employment and counselling services departments are identifying a greater need for career exploration and decision-making assistance for students and recent graduates.

Existing experiential career education programs such as co-op and practicum provide some job preparation information as well as work experience, but generally do not include any career exploration or career decision-making curriculum. In addition, these programs have limited accessibility. The recent economic downturn has demonstrated the volatility of the labour market and the need for university graduates to assume greater responsibility for their own career management.

The development and acquisition of career management skills are identified by the staff of career, employment and counselling services departments as a necessary complement to a degree; however this view is not necessarily shared by the academic side of the house and this is reflected in the absence of any career development curriculum in most universities and by the level of funding provided to the student services departments that deliver these services.

The shifts in the labour market from resource extraction and primary production to technology based employment have influenced the expectations and direction of the post secondary system. Course offerings have changed; computers are now integrated into programs or provide a technology platform for the course itself.

The general use of electronics in every day life has also had a profound impact on the delivery, and policies for delivery, of IGCS. The accessibility of information through the Internet has triggered and supported the movement to "E" government - with the use of technology and the Internet to deliver government programs, services and information. This impacts the delivery, of service to students and clients as well as the management of service delivery, with tools such as web based tendering processes. The use of Internet communication, e-mail, chat rooms, and news servers has also impacted coordination between governments, community stakeholders and service providers.

The wide range of issues identified reflects the diversity of stakeholders in IGCS, the different aspects of IGCS delivery in the public education, post secondary and employability programming systems, and the geographic differences in service delivery across BC. The complex lateral connections that exist within the broad area of career development and career search - regionally, nationally, and across sectors - make it more difficult to set clear goals and objectives, to raise the profile of IGCS and to ensure these activities are valued. The lack of a long term strategy may leave IGCS more vulnerable to the impacts of government reorganizations and changes in program directions or goals, and the shifting of staff roles or staff.

Organizational Issues

Organization issues identified include:

— A lack of clear responsibility for IGCS.

— A lack of clear objectives for IGCS.

— A lack of coordination between the different stakeholders.

— A lack of consensus of the skills, experience and credentials necessary for the provision of IGCS.

— A lack of coordination between government and industry to address current and future skills shortages.

— A need to address the challenges of the labour market.

— A need to address social issues.

— A need for incentive funds, grants and other mechanisms to encourage creativity at the community level.

Management Issues

Issues relating to the management of IGCS can be divided into labour market issues, awareness issues, human resource issues, information requirements and accountability related issues. Management issues related to the labour market include:

— The reality of the labour market - i.e. relative lack of opportunities - in local communities.

— The gap in services that support low skilled, uneducated workers, either directly or through employers

— The issues of rural life and isolation.

— The changing world of work and the need for continued education and access to education, including transitions for early school leavers.

— The skills shortage and how to market apprenticeship to youth and students.

— The need to make access and movement between institutions easier.

— The volatility of BC labour.

— The loss of government infrastructure such as ITAC.

Management issues related to awareness of IGCS include:

— A lack of the value or relevance of these services in long term labour market success for students and clients;

— The view that CAPP is not taught consistently in the secondary school system.

— The dissonance between viewing career transitions and career awareness as parts of core programming and the "back to basics" trend that focuses on traditional teaching areas.

— The lack of understanding that career development is a developmental continuum, not a fixed point of achievement.

— The need to encourage equity group participation in the development of IGCS.

— The view that career planning in colleges and universities is peripheral, rather than a core skill suffused into subject areas for students/graduates to manage their careers.

Management issues related to human resource management in IGCS include:

— The development and maintenance of effective core skills in counselling.

— The development and maintenance of the skills and knowledge necessary to integrate large amounts of information into an effective counselling/guidance/advising process.

— The need to provide ongoing professional development for practitioners. Some practitioners may have come into the field from other areas and have little or no counselling background.

— The need to develop equity awareness in IGCS practitioners.

— The need to develop a career track for career practitioners that reflects the value of this role.

— Government funding of short term projects is seen as a barrier to recruitment and retention of staff.

— The need to ensure that the diversity, of the workforce responsible for delivery of IGCS is representative of the diversity in the province's population.

Management issues related to information gathering and dissemination of IGCS include:

— The need for vast amounts of information on jobs, careers, training and labour market conditions that change frequently and vary widely across the province and country. This has implications for:

— The timeliness of information;

— The accuracy of information;

— The relevance of information at the community level and for local managers;

— The appropriateness of the material for various groups of people

— The lack of access to computers or to the Internet,

The success of IGCS at the individual level ultimately determines the success of programs and initiatives and continuation of funding for the service provider, so the effective delivery of services is critical. As there are a wide range of needs present within even apparently heterogeneous groups, the most pressing delivery issue is the ability to provide flexible services that address a variety of issues and needs, including:

— The readiness of individuals to access and use IGCS effectively.

— The need to address social issues that are not being dealt with, that IGCS alone can't address.

— The needs of different groups of immigrants and refugees with specific issues. Refugees, especially women, may have low levels of literacy; they may distrust authority and have a fear of accessing resources such as the police.

- The translation of information materials into a variety of languages.
- The adaptation of materials to allow for different cultural norms.
- The need for Qualification Recognition (QR) and Prior Learning Assessment (PLA) for new immigrants.
- The need for tailored training and learning opportunities for new immigrants; the individual may only need one component/course to be qualified, but the institution requires them to redo the full program.
- The lack of high school completion or low literacy levels of clients/students.
- The erosion of the social safety net, which may leave clients/students with few or no resources.
- The high number of single parents who are stressed or have few resources.
- The issues of poverty and especially child poverty.
- The need to address underlying drug and alcohol addiction, and the issues of dual diagnosis, where the person may have addiction issues and mental health issues.
- The need to address individual disability issues.
- The lack of transportation options, especially in rural areas.
- The lack of recognition by funders of the need to tailor services and the time it takes to screen or assess needs.

— The "digital divide" and the lack of access to technology.

There is a perceived lack of understanding that the practice of career development requires information to be integrated into a career and personal development process. Integrating information in this way is seen as creating relevance for clients and students. One example given is the opportunity to redirect youth who may otherwise become trapped into less socially acceptable validation groups such as gangs. This process is also seen in the context of learning, opening doors and connections to the community, and improving the quality of life for students and clients.

Policy Instruments

The importance of legislation in steering information, guidance and counselling services in BC. With the exception of the EI Act legislation does not play a major role in steering IGCS in BC. The Federal Employment Insurance Act - Part II, 1996, is the sole act that applies to British Columbia that specifically includes Information, Guidance and Counselling Services. The Act states that the "purpose of this Part [II] is to help maintain a sustainable employment insurance system through the establishment of employment benefits for insured participants and the maintenance of a national employment service."

It is the role of the national employment service to "provide information on employment opportunities across Canada to help workers find suitable employment and help employers find suitable workers." While there is no provincial legislation with direct jurisdiction over

Information, Guidance and Counselling services there are a number of ministries that have a direct interest in the provision of these services.

The relationship between government regulation, funding and provision of information, guidance and counselling services. For the most part, these activities are not implemented in a coordinated manner. Corresponding to the distributed responsibility for IGCS across a number of ministries and levels of government, there are only informal relationships between regulation, funding and provision of IGCS. This may result in policies that conflict or limit effectiveness.

Over the last ten years an informal system of networks between government and stakeholders has evolved to support the research, development, coordination, management and delivery of IGCS. While these networks are the result of working relationships between key individuals, they have also been supported and to some extent created by the two major joint initiatives between the Federal and Provincial governments, i.e. Strategic Initiatives and pilot activities under the Labour Market Development Agreement (LMDA). A wide variety of co-ordination mechanisms exist that may be formal in nature and ongoing, or project specific and time limited; they also take place at the provincial, local or area level.

Employer organizations play in the province - i.e. of funding, regulating and managing the provision of IGCS. With the exception of career-oriented web pages or links related to their websites, employer organizations do not independently fund IGCS. They do not play a role in regulating IGCS in the province, as IGCS is not a regulated activity per se. At times employer organizations and / or independent employers play advisory or management roles on IGCS initiatives funded by government or universities. While their role in terms of regulation, funding and management of IGCS is minimal, many employers and some employer organisations play significant reactive or responsive roles in IGCS initiatives at the community level.

There are a variety of ways that employer organizations are directly and indirectly involved in IGCS in BC. Whereas community and government IGCS services tend to be relatively client centred and involve a wide range of employment orientations, services provided by employer organizations frequently involve a marketing approach and are more narrowly focussed on particular fields. This is because employer organizations are either serving their own members, or attempting to attract individuals to their field of employment, or are serving individuals who have made a decision to explore employment opportunities in the sector. IGCS by employer organizations in BC takes the following forms:

— government / industry career information partnerships

— government / industry workplace-based training or matching partnerships

— experienced-oriented relationships with schools, universities and training bodies

— independent career informational activities of employer associations and employees

— development of position papers

These initiatives vary in scope and intensity but tend to emphasize information rather than guidance or counselling. Government is usually the funder, while the employer organization and/or individual employers provide the sector expertise and volunteers.

Employer involvement can be classified as "occasional", and is significantly oriented towards information rather than guidance or counselling. Although compared to the public and community non-profit sectors, union involvement in IGCS is modest, there are several ways in which unions do contribute to IGCS. Although not IGCS proper, in a general sense these contacts help legitimize the possibility of trades as a career path for students.

Community based service providers of IGCS are often an arm of a local society or not for profit organization that may have social or community goals in their mandate or constitution. These goals may include providing service to marginalized clients on the basis of need (not just the likelihood of success) and supporting families and communities. There was some concern raised at the dissonance of an organization striving for broader community goals while delivering services that have access limited by program criteria.

The need for information on jobs, labour market and career planning may be similar. However, the product and the medium of dissemination would be quite different for an educated individual with a visual disability and a youth with low literacy skills. Some of the ways IGCS are tailored to different target groups are:

— The inclusion of the family and ensuring informed consent when working with children and youth;

— The inclusion of local support groups for the target audience in the services;

— The inclusion of participation in community activities in the program or services;

— The inclusion of members of the target group population on the board or advisory groups;

— The inclusion of appropriate translations;

— The inclusion of appropriate materials;

— The inclusion of target group members in the development of products and services;

— The inclusion of the development of strong interagency supports for clients/students;

The major gaps, if any, in the provision of information, guidance and counselling services. It is extremely difficult to estimate the reach of services and the numbers and characteristics of students or clients served. This is due to the integrated nature of activities, the difficulties in tracking clients and the extent to which information is being delivered through the Internet. Without accurate information on who is being served it is difficult to estimate gaps. However, it is fair to say that when services are more accessible for those who are literate, computer literate and have access to Internet services then there is concern that a segment of the less literate population is left without service.

Gaps in services identified include:

— Access for low income individuals who are dependent on public access computers.

— Access for people who are neither in receipt of either IA nor EI, e.g. the underemployed.

— Access for those with the greatest need, as the current focus is on the most job ready.

— Access for those without post secondary training.

— Access to information and supports for those with severe learning disabilities.

— Access to career planning, job seeking skills and work experience placement for students with disabilities in the school system.

— Access to broadband Internet service.

— Access to materials in the client's first language.

— Access for aboriginals with disabilities.

— Access to pre employment training, life skills, or organized volunteering.

— Access to IGCS for university students.

— Access to information about opportunities within aboriginal communities.

— Access to post program supports for people who require job maintenance skills.

— Access to IGCS for university students and recent graduates.

Other gaps identified were of a broader nature. They included the need for more proactive and creative measurements of success. As measurement influences policy, this suggestion was seen as a way to develop policies to support a comprehensive approach to services. Labour market gaps were noted in jobs for people who like to work at tangible activities e.g. logging, fishing, and manufacturing. These people are not developmentally disabled, but do not do well when given analytical or theoretical tasks.

How information, guidance and counselling services are organised and provided for adults in your country. For targeted adults in BC, IGCS in both the Federal and Provincial "streams" are managed through government offices at the community or area level. The services are primarily delivered through community based service providers (including private and not for profit providers) on a contractual basis. The majority of IGCS are integrated into other services or programs offered by organizations, and therefore are difficult to quantify in terms of budgets or staff.

Youth and adults also have access to IGCS through the public post secondary system, and through the Internet delivery that is accessible although not necessarily targeted to youth. Students in post secondary institutions or alumni may also have access to services through on-campus career or employment services and through alumni associations or their university/college/institute.

Under the various Universities and Colleges Acts the Ministry of Advanced Education works with autonomous organizations and has no authority to set objectives or targets for linking activities such as IGCS. Rather the legislation enshrines the autonomy of these post secondary institutions. It is seen as the responsibility of the individual organization to develop the necessary steps, such as IGCS, that students require to become successful in their studies and make the transition to employment.

Three features characterize public employment service involvement in IGCS in BC:

— The majority of client-based IGCS services are contracted out to non-profit and private providers.

— The primary focuses of public employment services related to IGCS are the provision of career information, preliminary client screening, and referrals to service providers.

— The delivery of IGCS tends to be segmented, i.e. based on different target groups of different government departments and agencies.

The most significant in-house client-based public sector functions are those of training consultants and vocational rehabilitation services consultants in the Ministry of Human Resources. Training consultants meet with income assistance clients to assess job readiness, develop training and/or job search plans, and make referrals to employment-related training.

Depending on the skills and work-load of the training consultant, this role involves some measure of career counselling. Vocational rehabilitation services consultants serve clients with disabilities; their role can involve extensive assessment, counselling and resource development assistance. The other significant role of the public sector is the production and dissemination of career information. In the university and college systems, alumni associations, career services departments and/or counselling departments offer a range of career-related services to students, recent graduates, and alumni. These services vary from institution to institution, but can include:

— career fairs (sometimes co-ordinated between institutions)

— recruitment events

— workshops, lectures and job clubs

— individual career exploration and work search counselling

— career search internships

— on-line work opportunity postings and/or registrations

— on-line mentors

— career resource library, publications, and on-line access

— co-op education programs

— internship programs

Individual large corporations may provide career counselling to their employees. For example, McDonalds Restaurants states that career counselling is an integral part of its performance development system and are the responsibility of each department head. Career counselling by employers can also occur in industry sectors which are undergoing transition and lay-offs.

The private sector is involved in licensed product development related to IGCS. On the one hand these include large scale multi-national corporations such as Bridges, which targets schools, individuals and career practitioners throughout North America with a variety of assessment, experiential and training products. In general there are few formal processes of government specifically intended to encourage the provision of guidance and counselling services by private, for-profit organizations.

The non-profit sector plays a major role in IGCS delivery in the province. Non-profit IGCS deliverers are usually small scale community-based training organizations, but in some cases can involve as many as 100 or 200 employees employed in a variety of functions and locations in which IGCS may play some role. ASPECT is an umbrella organization of 120 career IGCS organizations in 58 communities. The majority of these are non-profits, with some private agencies and colleges forming the balance.

In general, the majority of non-profit community-based training (CBT) organizations serve clients with significant or severe employment barriers (e.g. Aboriginal clients, social assistance recipients, immigrants, persons with disabilities). A portion of staff time is often devoted to connecting clients with services for basic needs such as housing and transportation even before career issues can be addressed. In the CBT context career guidance and counselling is frequently part of a longer process of building client self-esteem, life skills and employability skills.

Approximately 90% of Employment Assistance Services (an HRDC program which helps unemployed individuals find and keep jobs through counselling, job search skills, job placement services and labour market information) are contracted through non-profit CBT organizations. Regulations of non-profit activities have increased in terms of financial accountability and outcomes through performance-based contracting. While supportive of quality controls, many non-profits see performance-based contracting as a problematic approach which insufficiently takes into account the greater level of effort needed to bring clients with significant employment barriers to a state of job readiness.

Furthermore, many non-profits feel that performance measured exclusively by rapid job acquisition and retention or by reduction in time on employment insurance actually works against thoughtful IGCS approaches. Performance-based funding is seen to encourage "cherry-picking" of job-ready clients rather than effort to help clients work through longer term approaches. Many nonprofits feel that, apart from some focus on the accreditation of private post-secondary institutions, there is negligible regulation of quality of service.

Career information, guidance and counselling services can be delivered in a variety of ways. Several generalizations can be made about these methods:

— Career fairs, some form of workplace experience, and (to a lesser degree) use of community members has remained consistent features of the IGCS landscape.

— The use of psychological tests, telephone IGCS services and educational transition years are not major features of IGCS in BC.

— Group guidance and counselling sessions and individual face-to-face interviews are still commonly used methods, especially in the non-profit sector, but in all sectors are subject to pressures for immediate placement of clients and for more self-directed approaches.

This growing orientation has resulted in the increased use of CD-ROM and Internet-based self-exploration, self-assessment techniques and the development of career information libraries. Several generalizations were made about Internet-based initiatives by respondents:

— information explosion - considerable time and expense has gone into the creation and linking of these resources, resulting in a veritable "explosion" of career information.

— information overload - while this increase in information resources is an asset, it can be difficult for practitioners to stay on top of all the resources so that they can be useful resource guides to their clients. Similarly, the endless maze of internet links and possibilities can be both time-consuming and confusing to clients.

— need for intermediaries - There is an appreciation that internet-based resources still require personal intermediaries in two forms: 1) persons to provide access to and assistance with navigating the resources, and 2) somebody to interact with. In regard to the former, there has not been a lot of research on how individuals access, navigate and use career information on the Internet. In regard to the second, several of the resources listed above have developed the capacity for interaction between users/learners and employers, mentors or coaches.

In British Columbia the public sector is a major contributor to production of career information, either directly in-house or via partnership and/or contractual arrangements with the (for-profit and not-for-profit) private sector. Ministries most actively engaged in producing career information include Education, Advanced Education, Human Resources and the BC statistical agency (BC Stats). In the last few years a number of these Ministries have collaborated together on a cross-Ministry basis and with the Federal Government (Human Resources Development Canada) to produce some very well recognized and used career information products and services in British Columbia.

Within the private sector a number of commercial interests also produce and sell various types of career information products and services. The most successful of these commercial interests (for instance, Bridges.com) market their products and services across Canada and to the United States. This (career information) market is largely unregulated with the exception of the primary and secondary school system, where the Ministry of Education may review and identify selected career information products and services as "approved learning resources" to be used with the official curriculum.

Almost all career information resources produced in BC are now available in print and on the Web. Notwithstanding the availability of most resources on the Web, print copies of publications are favoured by many practitioners and endusers. In addition, a significant number of the key web-based resources are also available in CD-ROM format.

There is a keen awareness of the need, and significant efforts have been made, to effectively segment the market for career guidance resources. The secondary school student making a transition to further education or to work is viewed as a major client for career guidance resources. Out-of-work individuals on employment insurance or income assistance are identified as another major client group to whom resources are specifically targeted.

In many cases, the career guidance practitioner is expected to mediate the information which is produced and substantial resources are directed towards supporting that process. Substantial and, in some cases, unique efforts are made to generate selected kinds of data which are used for purposes of developing career guidance information. For instance, occupational outlook information is derived from the Canadian Occupational Projections (COPS) model, jointly managed by a federal, provincial and territorial partnership.

Within BC significant resources are also allocated to initiatives to capture data on labour market outcomes of postsecondary graduates for use in career guidance publications. In other cases, data and reports available from both the federal and provincial statistical agencies are used to develop consumer oriented labour market trends and related information.

Modelling, survey and related results used in a wide range of career guidance information products and services are all maintained and updated on a regular basis by the responsible Ministries. Because development of many of the available career guidance information resources is funded by the two levels of government a substantial quality control and assurance process is in place and resources are reviewed on a fairly frequent basis and maintenance and updates scheduled accordingly.

In most cases, the process of developing career guidance information resources by governments has involved the use of appropriate user-needs analyses, including evaluations of earlier resources, user-needs assessments for new resources, focus groups, web traffic reports, and related. In general, it is a requirement that the information needs of a particular audience be established before a product or service is developed.

Major career guidance information resources produced in hard-copy or CD-ROM by government in BC are almost always (unless targeted to a very specific audience) distributed at no cost to secondary schools, post-secondary institutions, government employment and related services field offices, public libraries and private sector (usually notfor profit) employment services agencies. These same resources are usually also available for purchase by other agencies and individuals on a cost-recovery basis from the designated government supplier.

Almost all of the resources now available in print are also available on the World Wide Web in regular .HTML and/or PDF formats. In this case, both levels of government in BC have co-operated to support several private, not-for-profit web sites at which these materials are posted.

Within BC significant efforts are also being made to develop and use more regional, community based information for career guidance information purposes. The argument is simply that individuals look close to home first for information on employment, learning and related opportunities. There has been a major policy shift in the province since the change in government in 2001. The previous government saw funding as a tool for social change, and thus tended to emphasize targeted funding (e.g. through envelopes) for particular equity groups. The current government is moving rapidly towards funding based on performance criteria (e.g. labour market outcomes). This has meant more funding by block grants, within which the institution (e.g. school or college) has discretion to allocate funds in a way that is perceived most likely to meet the performance criteria.

Respondents identified a number of steps that government takes to maintain and enhance the quality of IGCS; however they also noted the large number of stakeholders and systems involved in IGCS makes it problematic to establish and implement standards. The steps identified range from direct regulatory and procedural approaches to the provision of support for others' roles in quality assurance.

Career and Transition Services Framework

The Career and Transition Services (CTS) Framework will help young people to make successful transitions through school and between school and post-school destinations. The Framework draws together a range of effective strategies, programs and activities that education and training authorities, schools, community service providers, government agencies and industry bodies can implement.

It is a Framework that expands upon many of the concepts in the *Stepping Forward*—improving pathways for all young people 2002 Ministerial Declaration and Action Plan. The CTS Framework provides for a national environment in which young people are fostered and challenged. The Framework is a guide for all jurisdictions, as well as the non-government sector and other practitioners, when developing and progressing strategies for the transition years.

The Framework provides flexibility for implementing strategies in ways appropriate to organisational circumstances, priorities and resource profiles. The Framework emphasises the need to act collaboratively and was developed drawing on the collective experience and observations of governments, schools, community groups and industry. It provides for a menu of options that provide practical support options and recognises that many of these strategies are already in varying stages of implementation, while others are the subject of continuing exploration. The strategies are premised on the belief that young people achieve greater success in their transitions when there is shared responsibility across a range of stakeholders.

To make effective transitions through school and from school to further education/training and employment young people require access to information and suitably qualified people to assist them in making key decisions about jobs, courses and career paths, including access to careers advice which is informed by current labour market trends.

Before making and implementing decisions about careers, young people need to develop knowledge and understanding of themselves in relation to the world of work. This includes consolidating the skills required to learn further as well as recognising and developing employability skills through the course of their everyday learning at school, in employment and training pathways, at home and in the community. Satisfying the needs of young people is the driving force behind the design and operation of any system that provides such a service, and this service should be available to all young people from their first year of secondary schooling.

All young people connect with educational institutions and therefore schools and other education providers should take a leading role in any systematic and comprehensive approach to assisting young people in managing transition processes. Schools and agencies should work closely together to ensure that young people and their families are aware of the full range of supports and information services available to them.

Career and transition services that meet the needs of young people will:

— Provide general advice and support at those key transition points when guidance on career and educational issues is necessary to help them make decisions that affect their future;

— Provide them with opportunities to develop career planning skills, enabling them to effectively manage their pathways beyond school.;

— Provide comprehensive careers advice connected to job opportunities (including local opportunities) supported by information technology systems accessible at the local level;

— Follow them up as they move through school into post-school destinations;

— Link them to appropriate learning and work opportunities;

— Support them through mentoring, brokering or other appropriate assistance;

— Provide in-depth support for those at risk of not participating effectively in education and training;

— Provide integrated specialist support for those facing substantial, multiple disadvantages preventing them from engaging in education and training and provide them with access to a range of specialist services to overcome barriers;

— Connect those who have left school to education/ training, career and employment information and opportunities; and

— Acknowledge options that extend beyond school years and offer support for programs that combine education, employment and training.

Objectives of CTS Framework

The objectives of the Career and Transition Framework are to ensure that all young people, with the support of their families and communities, have access to services through and beyond school which assist them to:

— Make informed choices when selecting schools, courses and post-school opportunities;

— Connect education and training pathways with career choices and employment prospects (including self employment); and

— Access the broad range of community services and specialist supports available to them.

Career and transition services within the framework should be:

— Delivered by professionally trained and committed staff able to access an extensive school-community network;

— Overseen by school principals, working with the school and broader community, who should have the prime responsibility for ensuring that each young person has access to services, including follow up; and

— Supported by appropriate monitoring and tracking arrangements across service and institution boundaries so that young people can be followed up as they move through school into post-school destinations.

Principles

— The goal of transitions should be comprehensive, covering employment outcomes, social participation and active citizenship;

— Young people should be placed at the centre of transitions arrangements – giving them a strong role in both the design of any transitions arrangements, and ensuring that such arrangements place an emphasis on their managing and directing their own transitions;

— The need for inclusiveness—a variety of transitions arrangements, appropriate to the capacities and needs of various groups, should apply to all youth, including both those in school or who have left school. There should be multiple entry and exit points which give youth multiple opportunities;

— An emphasis on facilitation as much as possible, ie providing youth with support which builds their capacity for self-management and direction;

— The need for a shared vision and sense of ownership for youth outcomes at the local level;

— The need for partnerships at a number of levels. Local partnerships which allow for a variety of approaches to meet diverse needs and circumstances, need to be actively stimulated and strengthened. There is a need to create a common vision and a shared sense of ownership across all the players at the local level;

— The role of governments include supporting local partnerships between business, education, communities and community organisations with appropriate frameworks and systems that explicitly articulate a partnership approach. Governments should aim to ensure continuity and sustainability of approaches;

— The role of schools needs to be examined and articulated. There may be a need to explicitly focus on changing the culture of schools and their perception of their role of supporting transitions. Specific areas to be addressed include school culture, their capacity for adopting a facilitative approach which supports young people's self-management, and the need for career and transition support to be delivered by professionally trained and committed staff; and

— The value of assigning accountability for transitions and measuring outcomes. The outcomes to be measured could include participation in education, training, employment and active citizenship, or the extent to which a young person (having left school) has acquired the means to access another stage to economic and social independence.

Elements

The Taskforce is proposing a framework for career and transition services which education and training authorities, schools, community service providers, government agencies and industry bodies can implement in ways appropriate to their circumstances. This framework consists of the following elements:

— Every young person from their first year of secondary schooling develops a 'Learning Pathways Plan' which should be altered to reflect their developing understandings as they move through school and on to post-school destinations, addressing transition issues as they arise;

— The plan should be developed by the young person with support from parents, friends, teachers and others who might be significant in their decision making;

— The Learning Pathways Plan could incorporate curriculum choice, recognition of necessary skill development, proposed career pathways, appropriate transition to further education, training and employment opportunities; and

— It should set out the goals of the young person and their strategies to achieve them and be flexible enough to change as life experiences, access to information and decisions change in the course of the young persons' schooling.

— To provide early intervention support;

— To give every young person the opportunity to acquire a skills portfolio document to record the development of skills and competencies; and

— To enable all education providers to develop the school-community (including business and industry) partnerships required to underpin successful early intervention and transition strategies.

— To implement arrangements that bring a consistent approach to an individual's exit planning, counselling, monitoring and support for school leavers that includes:

  — Schools working with young people and their families to develop exit transition plans that outline the strategies for transition to post-school destinations. This plan should encompass a range of needs covering further learning, employment and welfare;

  - — The plan having the capacity to identify and support early intervention needs including those in non-education areas; and
  - — The plan being endorsed by the school principal.
  - — This includes developing a system that actively engages with the young person and follow up young people as they make their transition from school.

This might include:

- — Reintegrating early school leavers back into school;
- — Supporting transitions to vocational education programs, employment assistance and/or employment; and
- — Providing support through the initial phase of employment.

Career education has an important role to play:

- — Within compulsory education: developing self awareness, knowledge and competencies regarding the world of work, and making decisions and transitions; and
- – Within post-compulsory education: being provided with effective advice and guidance on educational options will help to better match individuals' learning choices to their interests, talents and intended destinations.
- — Young people will have opportunities to participate in a range of vocational education experiences, including:
  - — VET in schools programs;

— Structured workplace learning; and

— Community based learning.

This will refer to services that assist all young people at any point throughout their transition process to make educational, training and occupational choices and to manage their careers. It will include a wide range of activities including:

— Activities within schools to help students clarify career goals, understand the world of work and develop career management skills;

— Personal advice, guidance or counselling to assist with decisions about initial courses of study, courses of vocational training, further education and training, initial job choice;

— The organised and systematic use of community members such as employers, parents and peers to provide occupational and educational advice and information; and

— Print-based, computer-based or on-line services to produce and disseminate information about jobs and careers, courses of study and vocational training to help individuals make career choices.

Career information, guidance and counselling services will:

— Include the use of current industry based informatio

— Be provided in a variety of settings: not only educational institutions and employment offices but also workplaces and community settings;

— Be provided in a variety of sectors: not only the public sector but also the private and community sectors;

— Allocate an important role to informal and non-professional sources of information and guidance such as local employers, community members, parents and peers as well as the formal professional sources;

— Play a pro-active role, helping individuals to create new options, as well as skills matching into existing jobs and courses. This implies:

  — Advocacy on individuals' behalf, and support for their self-advocacy on their own behalf;

  — Feedback to learning providers on learners' unmet needs; and

  — Encouraging and supporting the skills of career management, not simply facilitating initial educational and occupational choices.

  — Young people will receive efficient and effective help to secure and retain a placement in education, training or work suitable to their individual needs.

  — Young people may also need access to a range of services such as accommodation, access to alternative education and training, counselling and advocacy.

This will ensure approaches such as mentoring and case management are available for young people who would benefit from more intensive one to one approaches. These approaches will ensure:

— That early recognition of issues for 'at risk' young people can be reflectively responded to and addressed; and

— Practical local packages of support for young people with high support needs are available.

— This will ensure appropriate arrangements across service and institution boundaries so young people can be followed up as they move through school into post-school destinations. A monitoring and tracking system will:

  — Help identify students who become vulnerable or potentially at risk of not making successful transition;

  — Assist schools to assess achievements in supporting young peoples' transitions and report on these to their communities; and

  — Provide a basis for evidence-based planning (assisting schools, community groups and the department to refine programs and services).

This will include planning and developing (in a systematic way) a comprehensive IT based system:

— To act as a base-level universal statistical monitoring system for young people from their first year of secondary schooling that allows school principals to report on, and individual communities to assess, the success of local transition achievements; and

— To act as a local monitoring tool to ensure that all young people can be followed up and given appropriate transition support, including case management across a number of services and agencies where this is required.

Local Support Networks

Community Partnerships should be utilised to build Local Support Networks to implement the Career and Transition

Framework. This approach recognises the responsibility of the community as a whole to work together to support young people in their transitions from school to further education, training and employment. Principals will work closely with Local Support Networks, with all partners negotiating, and agreeing, to roles and responsibilities for the delivery of services to young people from their first year of secondary schooling. In signing off on the school exit plan, principals will ensure each young person has the opportunity to access appropriate services.

Local Support Networks will streamline current services through the creation of a network of professional advisers drawn from a range of backgrounds. Their functions will include:

- — Supporting the development of the Pathway Plans with young people and their families;
- — Supporting initiatives to make schooling more relevant for all young people;
- — Supporting all students to negotiate a school-to-work or further education or training Exit Plan;
- — Facilitating the follow up of all school leavers;
- — Facilitating the brokerage of placements;
- — Facilitating school-based mentoring arrangements; and
- — Referring ongoing brokerage and case management to appropriate people located in other agencies to ensure continuity.

To inform the planning of services, Local Support Networks will identify numbers of young people at the regional level with the following needs:

— Relevant and appropriate information and advice on education/ vocational, health and social issues;

— In depth guidance and support including the out of school population; and

— Sustained, integrated specialist support and tailored provision for those hard to reach and engage.

— Local Support Networks will outline the range and concentration of services to meet the needs of young people including ready access to information, guidance and transition support including:

  — A network of appropriately qualified advisers sufficient to meet identified needs;

  — Delivery mechanisms showing how existing resources are to be used;

  — Improving data sharing to enable efficient operation of services to be developed;

  — Ensuring the commitment of all organisations involved in the delivery of services;

  — Involving young people, their parents and the range of business/industry and community organisations in the development of services; and

  — Working with local providers to develop strategies to match provision to the needs of young people.

— Local Support Networks will support young people including those who are disconnected from schooling or at risk of leaving school early, by strengthening their abilities to make successful transitions to post-school options.

— Local Support Networks can be initiated within Community Partnerships by bringing together key agencies committed to supporting young people and their families and enabling them to:

— Set their own locally relevant objectives within an agreed Career and Transition Framework;

— Design their own advisory and planning structures that would be empowered to initiate local project development and delivery;

— Design and operate their own local action structures; and

— Pool the expertise and resources of local, state/ territory and national bodies, initiatives and programs to support local activity.

The approaches developed through Local Support Networks should have the following elements:

— Access to the information that young people and their families need when making key decisions about skills, courses, employment and career paths;

— Regionally specific information about education and training options, possible career paths, employment opportunities and current labour market statistics;

— The transition process has young people and their families as the drivers, navigators and decision makers;

— Every young person receives professional and ongoing transition advice beginning with their first year of secondary schooling;

— Schools take a systematic and comprehensive approach to assisting young people in managing the transition process;

— Transition advice services provided in schools ana the local communities will follow up all young people as they move through school into post-school destinations; work with school community partnerships to link each young person with appropriate learning and work opportunities; support each young person with appropriate learning and work opportunities; and support each young person through mentoring, brokering or other appropriate support;

— Young people who have left school have access to education, training, career and employment information; and

— Schools and community agencies work closely to ensure that young people and their families are aware of the community, government and industry information services available to them.

Due to complexities of life increasing day-by-day, the need for expert help is on the rise. Educational and vocational probloems form the main plank where counselling can expand in a big way as the scope is indeed very vast. Educational frontiers are expanding their horizons and it has become well-nigh impossible for students to make a choice of courses and careers without expert guidance. The students at the school exit level lack decision making on choice of further goals. This leads to th r failure in forming realistic life goals and plans. They lack both focus and meaning- ful direction. Often, they lose their way in the dark labyrinths of adolescence and do not know how to act or react.

The young lot comes across a number of problems that arise out of living with and sharing facilities with peers. Surveys on them have revealed widespread dissatis-faction and cases of depression in college and university level students. Provision of guidance and counselling services in the colleges and universities cannot be seen as a panacee for all our educational problems but it does offer the students a reasonable trouble free life. Our educational system also suffers from a number of defects. Least sought after subjects like humanities and arts are most offered and accepted, at college and university level. The young students needs to be informed about avenues that would become avoilable to then on completion of studies before hand. They need to be helped in making meaningful occupational selection and suitable preparation for entry into them. The average pass percentage at graduate and post graduate level is slightly above fifty percent. The failed ones often fall by wayside due to poor system of education and more often due to lack of proper guidance. It is in this regard that counselling services assume importance.

6

Guidance and Counselling: Ethical Reflections

Philosophical practice is, first, doing philosophy dialogically. Its status as dialogue is prior to disagreements as to its therapeutic uses, its potential as a service, and its being a way of life. Because dialogue, unlike private thought, presupposes an interlocutor, philosophical practice's adherents share the problem-at once practical and theoretical-of finding people with whom to do philosophy. Among the many questions raised by this circumstance, several are of first importance. Because the presence of an interlocutor stands as a necessary condition of the activity of doing philosophy dialogically, consideration of the circumstances of philosophical thought becomes a characteristic concern of philosophical practice in its more theoretical moments.

Inevitably, these considerations include the physical circumstances of the face-to-face encounter of philosopher and interlocutor. Philosophical practice's characteristic concern with the circumstances of embodied thought becomes a bias with respect to the practical philosopher's reception of philosophical work generally. Naturally, this bias will be most evident in approaching work that makes claims as to having import for how we lead our lives. The bias will be most evident in response to philosophers who have something to say about philosophy itself as it relates to the conduct of life.

There are three reasons for considering the category of the professions as a source of interlocutors for philosophical practice. The first is a methodological point. The concreteness of dialogue as a mode of doing philosophy simply makes it appropriate to consider the particularity of interlocutors where that information is germane to the understanding possible in the conversation. Second, Epicurus notwithstanding, it is not at all clear that everyone ought to do philosophy. This is not to suggest that some could be harmed by thinking, but simply that the benefit may not be universal. Members of the professions, on the other hand, are expected to be self-conscious or self-aware in their practice in contrast, say, to technicians, in a manner that is obtained in philosophical practice. The third reason for considering the professions is their embodiment of both technique and praxis.

Jaako Hintikka refers to the "paradigm of the craftsman" in commenting upon the ascendancy of the technical as the general model of rationality in the history of Western civilization. Hintikka explains the attraction of techne to the Greeks in terms of its clearly definable products as standards of success. Standards are of use only where there is the possibility of control. It is well known that the Greeks were much impressed at man's susceptibility to luck (tuche). In this connection Martha Nussbaum refers to techne as "a deliberate application of human intelligence to some part of the world, yielding some control over tuche."

Joseph Dunne has observed as a weakness in Aristotle's concept of techne that it fails to account for the exigencies of particular circumstances. Dunne notes that Aristotle does indeed address the problem for the application of techne in indefinite circumstances.

To exclude thought is not to exclude at least some of the feedback that Dunne argues is missing from Aristotle's analysis of techne. Certainly, response to the information of perception - however variable from one instance of execution to another - is internal to the execution of technique where it is automatic. What is excluded is judgment - roughly deliberation regarding the ends of the application of technique, and judgment is the domain of practice.

Judgment is decision as to whether technique ought to be applied at all. Since it is not internal to technique, which presupposes fixed ends, deliberation regarding ends is excluded from a purely technical rationality. Technical rationality is characterized by deliberation as to the most efficient means of accomplishing a given end. Hence Gadamer's image of the "monstrous arm" of technology whose enormous reach is obtained at the expense of genuine practice. It is not Luddite ranting that Gadamer offers, but critique of the technologizing of choices which otherwise offer opportunities for reflection.

A primary aim of ethics courses that use such cases is to enable students to identify ethical issues in their own practice, a condition clearly necessary before refection can be brought to bear on their resolution. Typically, however, the identification of moral issues is understood as the task of distinguishing them from technical, legal, or other categories of problems with which they might be confused.

There are two probable lines of response to this observation from the point of view of conventional ethics instruction. The first would be simply to accept it. While not seeing the shift in perceived burden of proof may be cause for regret, since it was not an actual occasion for decision, there was no moral issue. A second form of response would consider cognitive or organizational strategies by which one could be made more sensitive to conditions under which such oversights occur. The Challenger case is often cited as an instance of "groupthink", for example. One might also be made aware of the cognitive schemas by which we tend to organize information in practice.

From a perspective which distinguishes technique from practice, both forms of response could be characterized as taking a technical approach to ethics in that they could be said to regard the philosophical contribution to ethical practice to be theory or knowledge that is applied to situations identified as requiring deliberation. The first finds no opportunity for ethical reflection because no prior occasion for deliberation is identified. The second is an attempt to ensure that such occasions are identified. Since the first approach amounts to resignation, let us consider the second.

The main problem facing any attempt to understand the contribution of either ethical theory or practical philosophy more generally as a resource for deliberations is that it presupposes a perceived occasion for deliberation. The initial ethical question is "What ought I to do?" This circumstance betrays the technical understanding of ethics as resource. Technical rationality is engaged exactly when it is determined the end afforded by the technique is to be realized. The problem is in missed occasions for deliberation that subsequently become occasions for regret.

Even those approaches that appeal to the resources of cognitive science tend to concentrate on their engagement at the point that on occasion for deliberation is discerned. But Aristotle, certainly, is arguing that moral deliberation is not susceptible to a technical approach. The alternative to which Aristotle and Gadamer appeal is phronesis. Gadamer appropriates phronesis into his own work with its identification as a paradigm of experience, experience that the pragmatists would identify as consummatory. Like the pragmatists, Gadamer's notion differs sharply from the notion of the passive reception of sensation that the epistemological tradition has inherited from the British empiricists.

On the face of it, this essential quality of experience whose possession characterizes the phronimos would appear to offer direction at the absolute limit of technical rationality that the Challenger case exemplifies. At the limits of technical rationality, Gadamer's concept of experience might appear to give the professional something to do - something to cultivate as at least an aspect of her expertise. This approach, of course, would be a mistake, as it looks to experience as a means. Gadamer's treatment of experience is worked out precisely in opposition to such a technical understanding. Still, it is reasonable to expect of a concept of experience something that would contribute to an explanation of competence and skill, being the traditional counterpart to expertise acquired through the assimilation of theory.

Gadamer's argument that the process of experience differs from inquiry in having openness or receptivity to further experience as its fulfillment, rather than knowledge, does more to show that knowledge is not expected to issue from experience than it does to show that further experience is. The parallel with knowledge acquisition is misleading. Knowledge is related to inquiry as a condition of success, while openness is not so related to experience.

The professions recognize that as professional and not mere technicians (technitai, or embodiments of techne) they are committed to the cultivation and exercise of ethical choice. The same expectation of them is made by society. As consideration of the Challenger episode reveals, the seductiveness of technique and the socially validated identification of technique with rationality generally can cause those in the professions to fail to see even when the ethical question ought to be raised. This condition is and ought to be troubling to the professions. It is particularly troubling because the nature of the problem is such that it is a failure to see a problem.

Since technique is applicable at the point at which the problem is identified, technique is inapplicable in this case. Self-understanding, certainly, can be expected as a product of phronetic dialectic subsequent to the insight of a failure of expectation. We learn of ourselves how we have responded and how we would prefer to have responded. Such reflection would also be the occasion to reflect further on the ends of one's profession and on the limits of professional capacity. One might hope that these reflections would make one better prepared for a similar situation in the future, but given the nature of the problem, hope is all that is possible.

To inquire as to the probable products of phronetic dialectic, on the other hand, while a natural response, is to consider phronesis from an instrumental perspective of means and ends - concepts largely alien to phronesis. Instead, what can be anticipated is a perpetuation of the fabric of phronetic experience itself. Self-understanding is a legitimate expectation after all, as self-understanding is coterminous with phronetic experience.

Philosophical practice appears at the point that we ask how the dialectic of question and answer can be realized. While conversation is the model of Gadamer's hermeneutic philosophy, what can it mean to recommend actual conversation as a means of realizing the phronetic dialectic?

Conventional ethics instruction in the professions shares with Aristotle that ethics purpose is not character formation. Both share the view that the beneficiary of ethics or practical philosophy will be the person - the phronimos in Aristotle's case - who has already assimilated the ethos of his community. The practical value of the study of ethics for the professional is supposedly to provide the conceptual resources necessary for reasoned decision exactly when character is insufficient. Since Aristotle rejects this possibility, what is the practical utility of his practical philosophy?

Aristotle's own response employs a not entirely unambiguous analogy of an archer. Just as the archer has a target at which he aims, so will one's life be better led by having knowledge of the good. Aristotle's point, I believe, depends on our seeing that archery is an activity in which the agent has his end in view continuously in the course of the activity. Now, it is not practically possible to keep the ultimate ends of one's life or even of one's profession in one's consciousness at each waking moment, but one's life will be better to the extent that one can.

Relative to the professed purposes of instruction in professional ethics, the expectations of Aristotle and Gadamer are comparatively modest. Yet, they should be more modest still. Moments of painful insight are endemic to human and, specifically, professional life. While these are essentially negative, their logical structure that Gadamer elucidates as being that of question and answer afford opportunities for edification. Just as the professional embodies the phronimos, so the philosophical practitioner embodies practical philosophy at the point at which the question (whatever it may be) is raised in a professional's own practice.

Gadamer clearly regards his own meta-hermeneutic work as practical philosophy. Truth and Method, then, is a work in practical philosophy. But the form of life of the contemporary academic philosopher is largely arbitrary. It is arbitrary that philosophical reflection as it actually occurs in our time is primarily a reflection on texts. What philosophy as reflection on texts obscures is the occasion for reflection and the embodiment of the thinker.

Both conditions are material for reflection on philosophical practice, and the first - the occasion for thought - is material to philosophical practice. Peter Barnett in his *introduction to Questioning Time sounds Gadamerian* when he asks "whether it is possible to begin to make sense, whether there is a philosophical account of beginning to make sense, and whether beginning to make sense could be recognized as doing something philosophical." Barnett conceives of a "pure philosophical initiative" that would amount to the "project of making sense of the present on its own terms."

Bush Counselling: A Holistic Model

In 1983, many Australian outdoor counselling programs have commenced and subsequently fallen under the economic rationalists' knife. By using an Australian 'flavoured' model, Bush Counselling. This process assists the young person to bridge the gap and transfer the learnings from the bush into the home, school or work place. This model follows an adjunctive process of both enrichment and therapy depending on the needs presented by the individual participants.

Participants' issues are fleshed out prior to the program in consultation with referral agents and on pre-program activity days with the individual themselves. Similar to the concept of Wilderness Therapy the natural Australian bush is the medium where the emphasis is on the individual participant's development rather than the group. The group context is used to provide the supportive conduit that allows the individual to work on her/his own personal issues. The group disbands upon completion and a network of individual mentors, who have earlier assisted the young person's involvement, is then harnessed to help with the follow-up of participant learnings back into their community.

The counselling model used on Project Hahn programs is based on a preventive community framework and therefore focuses on normative mixed populations while still including those at-risk, using a program plan of maturational development. Participant populations are not limited to mental health or medical referrals. Participants are not (unintentionally or intentionally) labelled as disordered, dysfunctional or pathological. The emphasis is on well being, rather than ameliorating disease'. The aim is not solely to make the unconscious conscious as in psychodynamic therapies.

Therapeutic approaches that promote healing may be implemented within this therapeutic milieu, but non-therapeutic behavioural or attitudinal changes may justifiably be the participant's personal goal. The model focuses on a developmental perspective with the target audience being adolescents and young adults. The broad programmatic goal is maturation: changing from helplessness to a greatly increased capacity for self help onto increasingly balanced independence/ interdependence, and from a preoccupation with the present to a perspective that encompasses the past and anticipates the future.

Additional attributes include moving toward an ability to plan and be immune to momentary frustration, as well as identification and emotional participation in a larger social stratum. A predominant feature of at-risk young people is that aspects of their maturational development have gone into hibernation. An overriding program goal is therefore maturational acceleration.

The Bush Counselling model and provides readers with an understanding of the theories, therapies and experiences that form the 'cornerstones' on which this model rests. This Bush Counselling Model therefore brings together the techniques and procedures of Inner Sanctum practice which incorporate salient features of the Outer Sanctum foundation.

The rocks around the rim of a fire provide the boundary from which the embers can coalesce.Like those rocks, the following theories form the collective basis from which the different aspects of Bush Counselling are melded together.

It is essential to understand the human developmental process and how it relates to the behaviour of the people with whom we work. Of prime importance is the consideration of the developmental stage of the individual. Developmental theorists believe that each stage of human development involves a transition phase centred on a dialectic conflict. If each of these crises is resolved successfully, the individual able to move on to further growth and development.

For those who fail to achieve these developmental tasks, a level of confusion arises and the crisis is relived over and over. Marcia suggests four possible alternatives that occur as a resuit of the crisis of identity. For young people to develop a healthy sense of their own identity in an external environment that changing constantly, extreme resilience and high level of commitment is required. This apparent powerlessness to influence their world can lead to disillusionment and increasing numbers of adolescents find they lack the commitment or the desire to make the difficult choices to secure their personal identity. Often the result of this indecision lessens the potential for personality development and the individual fails to resolve the identity crisis.

Some individuals put the decisions on hold (moratorium) and allow themselves time-out to contemplate their options. An implicit understanding of lifespan theories enables a clear differentiation between thoughts and behaviours that are entrenched from those which are symptomatic of a specific developmental stage. This implies minimal concern for behaviour of a developmental nature; however, this is not the case. A prominent feature of this approach is the targeting of high-risk life styles led by adolescents.

Formal operations is the final stage of Piaget's cognitive theory and likely to occur during the early adolescent years. However, recent studies have demonstrated this level of reasoning may not occur belatedly and sometimes not at all, requiring the counsellor to reason in terms with which the group comfortable. If this risk taking behaviour is the result of the personal fable effect (ie. the adolescent feeling of indestructibility) alluded to by Elkind then timely intervention can accelerate the pace of maturation, where this egocentric behaviour may be discarded sooner.

By reducing their exposure to risk, the individual, the family and the community as a whole are spared considerable pain that is the consequence of a high-risk life style. This intervention can be made using an experience that enables the young person to experiment with elements of risk in an environment where a large contrast exists between the perceived risk and actual risk. Through timely Bush Counselling it is believed that the actual risk can be diminished.

Behaviourist Theory

An important assumption of this theory is that learning can improve problem behaviours. It has a strong goal emphasis that encourages the individual to actively work on changing his/her behaviour. This approach by its apparent flexibility and wide variety of therapeutic interventions. Two areas of development that are strongly represented in Bush Counselling are the radical behaviourism of Skinner and the social learning theory of Bandura.

Skinner argues against the humanistic ideas of self-determination and freedom suggesting that environmental reinforcers are the sole factors that motivate humans to change their behaviour. Social learning theory on the other hand rejects this view of human behaviour being linked exclusively to environmental determinants and suggests that individuals do have the capacity to influence their environments.

Skinner advocates a process called operant conditioning whereby learning cannot occur without some type of reinforcement, either of a positive or negative nature. Therefore behaviours that are reinforced with a negative consequence are less likely to be repeated than behaviours that attract positive reinforcement. The uncertain nature of the bush environment invites young people to experiment with different behaviour. This behaviour is reinforced by environmental determinants that reflect either a negative or positive consequence.

Bandura's efforts paved the way for inclusion of a cognitive process into his learning model. He emphasised modelling as a key means by which humans learned to master new behaviours. This is especially significant for work in the bush where group members can learn effective behaviours through imitation and observing each other in action.

Brief Therapy

The unpredictable nature of the bush lends itself to the principles of brevity that are part of solution-focused therapy. One goal of this approach requires resolution of the person's problem to be negotiated within a definite timeframe. Solution-focused therapists look to change as ongoing and resolute. Life is change and change is inevitable, and from this perspective, change is something that people either proactively choose or something that will happen regardless.

The interaction is short, as the focus is on the issue being presented. The purpose is therefore, not to understand the cause, but rather to find fertile ways of thinking about it and practical ideas to deal with it. In this way the solution is found in the future, rather than delving in the past, with resources used to create solutions rather than wasting energies on understanding the problem.

Subtle differences from traditional counselling approaches include the seeking of descriptive rather than interpersonal material, a participant action orientation rather than an insight orientation, and specific instead of longitudinal goals. This includes looking at the core messages in the essence of the story being told, as well as utilising positivity and participant's strengths to find personal solutions in the area of weakness.

Existential Therapy

Existential therapy highlights the freedom of individuals to shape their own destiny against a backdrop of human suffering that stems from living in a meaningless world. An important concept of this therapy is that anxiety is a normal condition of existence. In our daily lives, anxiety needs to be confronted if we are to push ourselves into new territory and change. This therapy has useful applications for the person confronting the existential questions that accompany developmental crises and fits well with young people who are questioning the meaning of life.

The basic therapeutic goals are to help people realise their freedom to become aware of their potential, to challenge clients to accept responsibility for the events in their lives, and to discover the past decisions that are keeping them from discovering the true meaning of their existence.

Person-Centred Therapy

Like existential therapy, person-centred therapy (humanism) focuses on the phenomenological world of the individual and the modelling of authentic behaviour to group members. By accepting that each person structures themselves according to their own perceived reality, the practitioner has a fundamental need to enter that subjective world. The focus of therapy away from traditional instructive and interpretative roles allows the counsellor to concentrate fully on what is being conveyed and to respond authentically.

Carl Rogers believes that a person knows himself or herself better than anyone and through growing self-awareness will make self-discoveries that reshape their world. The emphasis of person-centred therapy is on helping the client learn to listen to themselves and engage in a more congruent life style. This style creates a caring and empathic tie not only between the practitioner and the group but it also influences interaction between members themselves.

The use of active listening skills forms the basis of counselling sessions recognising that few participants ever have the opportunity to be heard without judgement. Young people are usually keen to talk honestly about themselves and unlike many other therapies the person is in the driver's seat throughout the session.

Gestalt Therapy

By leaving the emotional lessons young people learn to chance, we risk largely wasting the window of opportunity presented by the slow maturation of the brain to help cultivate a healthy emotional repertoire. Taking ownership and responsibility for emotions and behaviour can be risky business. Emotional healing requires the courage to take chances, to experiment with new behaviours, to feel emotions in their intensity, and to move toward a better understanding of self.

The way forward is to face anxiety, which often takes the form of resistance, rather than to take flight from it. It means experiencing all the things about to occur in their fullness, the entire range of emotions. The counsellor helps to provide the sanctity necessary for this freedom of emotions to surface. The participant should feel free to be angry, sad, happy... and to fully experience her/his authentic self. Specific techniques are not the focus of the counsellor but rather it is the philosophical framework that the different techniques provide.

In Bush Counselling the activities are simply the medium which allows participants to work on their personal issues within a supportive group environment of which they have volunteered to participate. Its action-orientation is more conducive to adolescence emotional growth than the adult structures of traditional counselling. Acting out unresolved feelings in the relative safety of their newfound peer group supports the risk involved, and meets the energy levels and social needs of this population.

Inner Sanctum

The following counselling approaches and therapies are

drawn from a combination of the theories noted earlier. The campfire metaphor of burning embers represents the vibrant fire, and the 'aliveness' of these approaches. The Piagetian concept of disequilibration is the conflict experienced by an individual when forced into a process of adaptation. Activities that involve a high level of perceived risk allow the individual to experience heightened awareness of the disequilibrating process, encountered prior to successful completion.

At the edge, self-defeating internal dialogue builds up and gets louder, changed physical characteristics become obvious and emotionally the individual is often intensely fearful. Bush Counselling programs involve a healthy alternative to challenge and risk, which for many young 'substance users' are important parts of their life. The nature of the experience requires commitment to the process and often members have few options other than to continue the experience.

An example of this is designing a bushwalk route to include major difficulties toward the latter half of trip. When group members consider the options, they see the way ahead as uncertain though preferable than retracing their steps of the last few days.

Experiential and Heuristic Learning

Learning from experience is the process whereby human development occurs. L. S. Vygotsky Self-learned heuristic principles are linked strongly to self-motivated learning within the structure of the wilderness program. A key element in humanist and solution-based approaches is for the participant to be in control of her/his own counselling. Individuals the freedom to react and challenge in any way they feel is appropriate and responsible during a wilderness experience. Thus, it is believed that on-going positive future behaviour has more likelihood of success through heuristic learning than if subtle advice is offered.

The learning heurist is a great friend to the wilderness counsellor for it provides free of charge a tool of self-determination that operates independently of the counselling relationship. This often happens in wilderness programs where the experience is left to speak for itself. An example of this approach is the orchestrating of an experience for an individual or group that provides a timely and specific learning.

Heuristic learning is hastened immeasurably through the use of handicaps. This method limits the ability of the participant to use their natural strengths and invites them to use less certain strategies to achieve their goals. These uncertainties bring with them a disequilibrating tendency to which the participant responds by attempting to find ways to adapt to the new environment. The range of learnings that stem from this process can be expected to better equip the individual with an increased repertoire of coping mechanisms that can be integrated into their lives post-course.

An unduly dominant leadership style can encourage co-dependency counter to the fostering of independence and promoting of empowerment central to existential, humanist, and solution-based therapeutic goals. A key ingredient in this leadership style is non-directive intervention which gives the individual the control of making her/his own mistakes and finding her/his own solutions.

Gestalt therapy recognises that the developmental progress of every group is important to consider and carefully monitor before disclosure can occur safely. It may seem paradoxical that a community that is built around safety is an appropriate haven for conflict. To make the most of the opportunities presented for individual emotional depth, the counsellor has to attend closely to the group needs. Modelling sensitivity and inclusion of all group members are essential practices used to bring the group together. Only at certain stages of group development is it appropriate to include activities and discussions that require trust. This requires flexibility of program structure so that adjustments can be made for different groups.

The counsellor's prime focus is to establish a common ground for communication to occur. This can come about by modelling feelings of discomfort to gain the group's confidence. Active listening and providing for their needs goes a long way toward maintaining a friendly atmosphere.

The need to belong, the need for relatedness is a key requisite for members of the group experiencing Trotzer's second stage. The desire to be a part of the group is a motivating factor for acceptance of each person regardless of their behaviour exhibited outside the group. The counsellor's behaviour therefore needs to reflect this through modelling the acceptance of behaviours and attitudes. Rogers terms this acceptance as unconditional positive regard.

The counsellor encourages individuals to maintain focus on their solution to problems by modelling self-responsibility. This is achieved by demonstrating that the facilitator's weaknesses are recognised and can be talked about non-defensively to members of the group. An example of a question that might be asked at this stage is,

"What do you need to do yourself to solve your personal issue?"

Work stage of group development comes later in the program, involving open discussion of personal issues and creating an atmosphere where alternatives can be tried and examined free of threat. This is the moment when individuals can try out new behaviours or attitudes in a safe setting prior to risking changes outside the group. The facilitator's role here is to model vulnerability by actively seeking solutions to problems and asking group members for assistance.

The realisation that something of great significance is coming to an end elicits a sense of sadness in the group. Participants take credit for their own changes, yet the difficult task for each person is modifying behaviour and attitudes outside of the group. People outside the group may not give encouragement or reinforcement to the member for acting in new or different ways. Without a source of support, the chance of regression to old ways is greater.

Social norms agreed to by the group prior to the start of the program greatly assist all members to establish ground rules for monitoring appropriate and inappropriate behaviour. Boundaries as noted by behaviourists act as a liberating force allowing the space and security for young people to work on their issues. In Bush Counselling three simple points cover extensively the issues that are likely to arise. The giving and receiving of feedback is a useful tool in allowing people to consider changing their behaviour.

If the feedback is offered constructively the person receiving it is more likely to hear it without becoming defensive. The second point is no 'put downs' to others or yourself. This includes accepting differences within the group and becoming aware of negative self-talk that may influence personal endeavours to get the most from the program. The third, a very important facet of Gestalt Therapy, is that all group members respect the physical and emotional safety of self and others. Only without fear of criticism or rejection can the individual begin to explore new territory.

There is a need to openly evaluate the spiritual aspects of wilderness programs and to highlight the connections between spiritual strength and the development of individual well-being. Frankl suggests that often it is an extremely difficult external situation that gives humans the opportunity to grow spiritually beyond themselves. The tough experiences encountered on a wilderness journey have an impact on participants' spiritual development but linking this back into the home environment is necessary to increase their definition of themselves within the constructs of their relationships and communities. Often this is done in a reflective way through a solitary meditation exercise or simply one-on-one during the day's journey.

Brief therapy holds that the participant is the best therapist when it comes to finding a solution to his/her problem. Approaches to help them find a solution may lie in externalisation, miracle questions or scaling. When an adolescent holds self-defeating views of her/himself and is totally overwhelmed by the problem then a process of externalisation can help them lessen the impact. By separating the person and the problem, a space is created whereby she/he can gain some control over its influence.

Scaling is a useful monitoring tool that can be implemented to gauge feelings, physical effects and general well-being in the group. Its greatest application for Bush Counselling is in the monitoring of personal goals. Heatherton and Nichols, when studying people who had successfully changed a major aspect of their life with those who hadn't, found the 'changers' had invariably re-appraised their goals in life and increased their self-knowledge and understanding.

Personal goal-setting is central to behavioural therapy. When relating this to 'Bush Counselling we encourage goal setting at all levels, individual, group as well as practitioner goals. To create a climate ripe for change, selling the idea of personal growth to young adults is essential. For the young person engaged in the storm and stress of adolescence this may lack relevance, however a well fleshed out and measurable program of change is a key requirement of our work. This includes vigorously challenging young people on programs to formulate personal goals of significance, not just a non-specific aspiration dreamed up to placate the counsellor; to set the scene by modelling a personal goal that honestly describes aspects of your life with which you struggle; and that the counsellor too, has something significant to gain from the process.

This 'program of change' may house goals within goals and, using a ladder as a metaphor, each rung is viewed as a specific short-term goal leading to a change of great significance. Further the program of change stresses the need to constantly review goals on the basis that we all bite off more than we can chew at times and conversely encourage the formation of realistic goals requiring real effort and courage.

Wilderness programs use activities like abseiling that promote task mastery. Peer modelling can play a major part in this process, yet success can also be achieved with a supportive peer environment that encourages the individual to attempt the task because the consequences of failing are significantly diminished. Other strategies that can be adopted by both individual and counsellor are the re-evaluating of goals and the use of a staged approach to various challenges.

An example of this might be using three abseils of varying stages of difficulty to encourage a progressive approach to task mastery. This also highlights the need to assess the level of skills within the group and to fix the degree of difficulty to a challenging yet achievable level. Remoteness and attending to needs The counsellor's office, for some of the young people with whom we work resembles their school environment which may hold negative connotations, whereas the bush setting where we prefer to practise transmits a stimulating alternative clothed in uncertainty.

Central to all counselling theory is the need to provide a safe and secure environment in which to practise. Unlike the air-conditioned office, issues such as adequate warmth and clothing need to be addressed before individuals will focus on the lofty ideals of personal development and behavioural change. If their needs of survival and safety are being met, working with this person on issues relating to the needs of belonging or esteem will likely prove effective.

External reinforces, a cornerstone of Skinnerian approaches, is all but passe' in most post-modern counselling practices. Yet in the strategic use of risk-recreation activities such as bushwalking, caving, kayaking and abseiling, the external environment provides the individual the freedom to make choices. For the young person who has suffered from repeated failure, a successful abseiling experience reinforces the actions that enabled him/her to risk uncertainty and step off the edge.

Failure on the other hand is a valuable method of learning for both individual and group as it provides opportunities to change behaviours that are no longer effective. As a learning tool, future behaviours are influenced through the continued reinforcement of personal decisions which reap success and the subsequent extinguishing of behaviours from decisions that potentially cause discomfort.

Group Heterogeneity

All counselling theories allude to the metaphorical journey of change. The journey of a small group through a vast landscape allows for a strong sense of community to develop and through establishing meaningful relationships, individuals can come to know themselves. The opportunities for spiritual development are manifold in such awesome surroundings where the concerns of the world lack relevance in comparison. The action mode is integral to any bush journey and it is of great assistance to the Bush Counsellor.

Through involvement in the completion of tasks the participant begins to feel like he or she is in transition. A journey implies that action is involved as the impetus to reach a destination point. In the bush setting this destination is vague and murky and holds within it a sense of mystery and discovery. The passing of time changes as the journey progresses. It takes the participant some time to slow down and move at the pace dictated by the bush environment.

Counselling for Better Performance

The term 'counselling' is used in the sense of assisting people to achieve and maintain a satisfactory standard of work performance and should not be confused with the type of counselling provided by professionally qualified counsellors. Managers are not expected to be psychologists and they should not try to solve difficult personal problems which their people may experience. Employee Assistance Programs and staff counsellors have the skills to deal with such problems and managers should make use of these resources where appropriate.

Effective managers are good people managers. It is your responsibility to foster a workplace culture in which people can maximise and maintain their level of work performance. To do so, it is essential that you establish clear communication with your staff; counselling and feedback are two very important tools that you can use in that process. As a manager, it is your responsibility to continually monitor the way your staff are performing and provide them with appropriate guidance and support.

It is easy to take good work for granted and only provide negative feedback when something goes wrong. But if people are to feel that their work has value, their achievements must also be acknowledged. Regular, positive feedback can be a powerful tool to motivate and enhance the performance of your staff. The following checklist gives important characteristics of effective performance management.

— Managers provide leadership and integrate performance management with other aspects of their work in managing people.

— People understand that their performance directly contributes to the ongoing success and viability of their agency.

— Individual and team responsibilities and their performance are clearly linked to the attainment of program and corporate goals and the needs of clients.

— Individuals and teams have a clear understanding of their work responsibilities and the standards of work expected of them.

— Individuals and teams meet the standards of behaviour expected of public servants.

— Managers monitor and assess the performance of their people.

— Individuals and teams receive regular feedback on their performance against program and corporate goals.

— Managers make use of the potential of all their people and develop their skills in encouraging individual career planning.

— Improved and valued performance is recognised and rewarded.

— Managers seek to improve poor performance and address continuing poor performance.

Counselling and Feedback

The purpose of both counselling and feedback is to provide your staff with the information, advice and assistance they need to contribute fully to the achievement of your organisation's objectives and, where a person fails to make the required contribution, to demonstrate that you have made an appropriate effort to assist them. Many situations involve a combination of feedback and counselling, or a progression from feedback to counselling. For example, when assessing how a probationer is performing, you are expected to provide feedback.

If, however, despite having given the probationer an appropriate level of advice and assistance, you identify a problem with their work performance or conduct, you may also need to initiate counselling. The following are particular situations where counselling and/or feedback may be appropriate:

— as part of a regular system of performance feedback;

— assessing the performance of a probationer;

— in the context of performance appraisal;

— assessing staff training and development needs;

— in connection with a referee's report;

— after a selection process;

— if a person is planning to retire or resign from the service;

— where there is a decline in work performance;

— where the standard of conduct is not being met;

— where there has been particularly good performance;

— where a difficulty has been overcome; or

— to maintain continuing good performance.

Feedback is generally informal and involves you and your staff member exchanging information in a broad range of situations about how you can best work together to achieve the goals of your organisation. Feedback requires you to communicate clearly to the person what is expected in terms of work performance and conduct and regularly inform them of the extent to which they are meeting those expectations. Feedback ranges from oral comments on a person's performance to written reports, such as probation, performance appraisal or referee reports.

It is important for feedback to be a two-way process. Firstly, a feedback discussion should also give a staff member the opportunity to express his or her views on your performance. You need to receive 'upwards' feedback from your staff in order to accurately gauge how well you are fulfilling your own responsibilities. By giving consideration to upwards feedback you can reinforce the message that individual contributions to team performance are taken seriously. Secondly, if you have a concern about a person's work performance it is usually more effective to work with the person to develop a solution rather than attempt to impose one from above.

A co-operative, corrective approach will frequently achieve the best result. If feedback is balanced and constructive, your staff are more likely to respond to concerns about their performance with an effort to improve. To be fully effective, feedback should be:

— based on open, two-way communication;

— timely and regular;

— factual and specific;

— understood;

— honest;

— constructive; and

— followed up.

Feedback is more effective if given on a regular, continuing basis. It need not, and should not, be limited to structured processes. Any concerns you have about a person's performance or conduct should be addressed promptly. Early intervention can often prevent more serious problems developing. Similarly, good performance should be promptly recognised. You should focus on measurable performance. Avoid making unsubstantiated judgements. Give tangible, specific examples whenever possible rather than generalising. You should also ensure that any information that you provide, e.g. concerning entitlements, is accurate.

Your staff need to understand why you are giving them feedback: that their individual performance is linked to the achievement of corporate objectives. It is also important, if you identify an aspect of a person's performance that requires improvement, that you make the person clearly aware of the established standards and in what way you consider that they are not being met. When you talk to staff about their performance you should clearly articulate your reasons for doing so and outline possible action that may result if there is no improvement.

Problems may arise if managers and staff place differing interpretations on a discussion. In some cases a manager may feel that he or she has counselled a person while that person is under the impression that nothing more than a routine discussion has taken place. Inform the staff member prior to any discussion as to what issues you wish to discuss with them and give them an opportunity to discuss them immediately or make another time.

You should be honest, but not coercive or offensive. Frame the discussion around ways to improve performance rather than focusing solely on problems or perceived shortcomings. In many cases, even when a person is experiencing performance problems, there will be particular tasks which they still perform well.

Little will be achieved if feedback is not followed up. You need continually to monitor and evaluate the performance of your staff. When, following a feedback discussion, you agree on a course of action to improve a person's performance, e.g. to investigate the possibility of providing training or developmental opportunities, it is important that you follow up your commitment. It is equally important for staff to be committed to improvement and to follow up the actions to which they have agreed.

Some managers may tend to focus on the negative aspects of feedback. While it is important to encourage improved performance in those not functioning to the required standard, you should try to adopt a balanced approach by also recognising and rewarding good performance.

Formal performance appraisal schemes provide an opportunity to recognise and reward good performance. There are many other informal opportunities, such as annotating a person's work with positive comments, especially if those comments will be seen by senior management; taking a few moments at a meeting to acknowledge someone's good work; allowing an individual to take on more challenging and responsible tasks; or praising good work in the presence of senior management.

Performance problems can sometimes result from factors other than the capacity or willingness of staff. Limited resources, inappropriate job design and inefficient or outmoded procedures are among a range of things that may contribute to poor performance. Regular discussions with your staff will give them the opportunity to bring such factors to your attention, and they are likely to be more willing to accept the measures taken to address such problems if they have been able to participate in developing the solutions.

It is important for managers and employees to understand each other's needs. You should establish what your staff need to do their jobs more efficiently and your staff need to fully understand your requirements. A needs-based approach should help you to establish effective communication and thereby improve performance in your workplace.

Counselling is a formal process, initiated when a person has not responded to advice and assistance you have provided on a less formal basis, and will usually involve your taking the following steps:

— advise the person in advance that a discussion about his or her work performance or conduct is to be held at a given time and place, with sufficient notice to enable you both to come to the discussion prepared;

— arrange for the meeting to be held in private, although a support person for the person being counselled may be present, as well as someone you may have asked to attend as an observer; and

— keep a brief record of the meeting-this could be a diary note.

A good management style will not eliminate performance problems, but good workplace communication should help you to identify some problems early, so you can do something about them. In most cases it is your responsibility as a manager to provide counselling to your staff in relation to work performance and conduct. However, in circumstances where performance is affected by factors outside the workplace, for example if a person has a problem with drugs or alcohol or has difficulties in their private life, it may be appropriate, after an initial discussion, to refer the person to a staff counsellor or counsellor from an Employee Assistance Program (EAP).

This does not mean that you should back away from the problem, but you should focus on ways to improve the person's performance at work and not attempt to solve problems that may be occurring in the individual's private life. In most cases, managers are not qualified to take on such a role. Apart from providing a counselling service for staff, EAPs can also help you as a manager. For instance, if you are faced with having to give a person critical feedback about their performance and you feel uncertain about your approach, you may wish to contact the EAP to obtain advice on how to best frame the discussion. You may also wish to consult a more senior manager or contact your human resources area for advice.

In some cases it may be appropriate to involve a professionally qualified counsellor outside your agency, such as a medical practitioner. If you are considering an external referral you should not put pressure on the person to seek outside counselling. A referral should be arranged only with the person's consent. Generally, people should be praised in public and criticised in private. However, some people may be embarrassed by unexpected public praise, and so you need to be aware of this and use your own judgement when delivering positive feedback. It is advisable first to let a person know they have done a good job and then, for example, to tell them that you intend to mention this at the next meeting.

Where formal counselling is to be done, the discussion should ideally be held in a place which is private and free from distractions. Your office, if you have one, may be appropriate but, in some situations, a more neutral meeting place away from the immediate work area may be preferable. Where possible, a suitable time for the discussion should be agreed in advance and sufficient notice given to allow both yourself and the staff member to prepare adequately.

While it is desirable for a person to be given sufficient notice to prepare for a counselling session, there may be occasions when you decide that a person's behaviour warrants immediate action, particularly when the behaviour is causing disruption to other staff. A counselling discussion usually involves a manager or supervisor and a staff member but, in some situations, you may find that a person requests the presence of a support person or independent observer.

You may also wish to have an observer present. A person or persons attending a session in this capacity wouid not normally take part in the discussion and their presence and role should be clarified before the session commences. To achieve the best results, counselling, like feedback, should be based on open, two-way communication. You should work with a person to generate an agreed plan of action, establishing and articulating the needs of both the manager and the staff member. Focus on future outcomes rather than dwelling too much on what has happened in the past.

Your aim is to produce an improvement in the person's performance or conduct and for this to happen you should, first, agree that an improvement is required and, secondly, agree on the steps which should be taken to achieve it. It is also important that you establish a time frame to achieve your agreed goals and to review the success of your strategy.

If you initiate a counselling session in relation to underperformance or conduct you should keep a formal record as evidence for both parties of what has occurred and as a basis for future action. The record would also show that counselling has taken place, in case a formal process, such as the agency's procedures for poor performance, is later commenced. You should make the record as soon as possible after the meeting, while your recollection of the events is still fresh.

It will depend on the seriousness of the situation under discussion how much detail you record, but you should include relevant facts, such as the names of the people present, the date and location, the reason for the discussion and the main points covered, including the positives, and any agreed actions or outcomes, including time frames. You should not include unnecessary details about a person's private life. Recording information which is not relevant to the purpose may mean that you are in breach of the Privacy Act.

Both you and the person being counselled should sign the record, unless the person believes that the record is not an accurate reflection of the discussion, in which case he or she may attach their own signed version of the meeting. If other people are present as observers you should also ask them to sign.

You should inform the person that you have made a record, for what purpose, and who will have access to it. You are then responsible for storing the record securely, using an in-confidence file, and preventing any unauthorised access. Matters raised in a counselling discussion should be treated confidentially, and disclosed to third parties only in line with the relevant Information Privacy Principles. You should generally inform a person if you are disclosing or referring a record of counselling to a third party, except where this is for a routine purpose, explained to the person at the time of the counselling.

If you consider that a formal process, such as misconduct or underperformance, may be necessary, you may need to pass counselling records to your agency's human resources area. If, while you are reviewing a person's conduct or work performance, the responsibility for their supervision passes to another manager, it will usually be appropriate to pass on your records.

This is particularly important in cases involving misconduct or underperformance as in these cases there is a need to establish clearly what counselling and feedback have taken place. The processes can be unnecessarily prolonged if changes in supervision result in a lack of continuity in the recording of such action.

Good practice suggests that such records should be destroyed at the end of the two years unless further counselling or other action on the issue in question is required during that period. Where a record of counselling is placed on a personal file, e.g. if it relates to possible misconduct action, underperformance, the record should be retained as a basis for further action and to allow for periods of review. You should be aware that any records of counselling that you create may be required to be produced in legal proceedings.

The expected outcome of counselling is in most circumstances an improvement in work performance or conduct. If a person's conduct or work performance does not improve in response to counselling there are a number of options available. These include:

— re-arranging the person's duties;

— movement to an area where a person's skills may be better utilised;

— voluntary reduction in classification;

— procedures for dealing with underperformance; or

— misconduct procedures.

If you are considering formal procedures for dealing with underperformance or suspected misconduct, you should contact the human resources area of your agency for advice. It is essential to address problems with performance or conduct when they arise. If you use them appropriately the formal processes can be effective in dealing with underperformance and misconduct and produce an outcome which is efficient both in terms of maintaining productivity in your workplace and in reducing the negative effects of a protracted, unsatisfactory work situation.

Good practice suggests that, before any written warning is issued to a person about underperformance, counselling should take place, observing the following points:

— you should discuss the work standards expected of the person and provide appropriate assistance to enable the person to meet those standards;

— you should make clear to the person where their work is below standard and set goals for improvement over an agreed period;

— you should make records of counselling sessions, signed by both parties; and

— you should give the person the opportunity to explain any reasons for underperformance.

Client-Centered Counselling

Beginning in 1993, counselor training curricula were revised to reflect the shift from an information-based education model to a more interactive and "client-centered" use of counseling skills. However, the institutional culture of the CT program has not been able to accommodate the new model of interaction.

Clients are interrogated and patronized while their sexuality is ripped out of context and plotted against a highly clinical grid of time, risk, and latex. It would be difficult to imagine a less "client-centered" form of interaction. Counselors employ a number of distancing strategies in order to mitigate the impact of the questions. Perhaps the most common strategy is to simply resort to the didactic model of counseling in which an expert provides information to a passive client. In this context, the bureaucratic and impersonal format serves the interests of both client and counselor in speeding the process along with minimal friction.

Clients spoke very little compared to the counselors. In the rare instances when the client expresses fear or anger concerning their situation, counselors either changed the topic, abruptly turning to the next question on the form, or provided vague reassurances. Based on the counselor's follow-up questions, the client's narrative appeared valuable to the counselor only to the extent that it provided information required by the form. Counselors routinely repeated questions for which the client's narrative has already provided an answer.

Instead, counselors spent the bulk of the sessions explaining the testing process and completing the form and the related lab slips. Each counselor provides his or her own standard checklist of information that varied little, if any, between clients. Clients asked few questions, and the length of the sessions varied primarily according to the amount of information or advice the counselor typically presented. Additional training is often advocated as a solution for counseling that diverges from expected standards. Certainly, more training and continuing education can only help.

Test Counselling

Test counseling is a unique and unprecedented behavioral intervention that is still in search of a standard of practice and transtheoretical model. Test counselors receive minimal training: a three day introductory training, a two day follow up at six months, and annual continuing education updates where available. To justify this low level of training, program administrators claim that counselors are "selected" rather than "trained." Many counselors are volunteers, nurses, or medical assistants, and the vast majority lack professional training in counseling or behavioral research.

Most test counseling occurs in clinical settings where time-intensive, mental health issues are generally given a low priority. In this context, counselors are more likely to be selected for their blood drawing skills than for their interpersonal skills. Whatever communication skills counselors have learned through socialization and bring to their work, the skills needed to confront risky behaviors require counselors to act in ways that are somewhat "anti-social". Often, trained counselors employ various techniques to confront, challenge, or even empathize with clients in ways that depart significantly from nromal conversational dynamics.

It is crucial for counselors to have a clear understanding of the standards and limitations of their role in primary prevention. During the initial phase of the CT program, from 1985-1987, HIV testing was originally conceived as a way to protect the blood supply by diverting high-risk clients away from blood donation centers and into "Alternative Test Sites" (ATS). During these years, test counseling was mainly conceived in terms of crisis management for the large numbers of HIV positive clients.

In San Francisco in 1987, the proportion of positives was 20%. Counseling was provided at the post-test, and groups of clients watched a video in lieu of a pre-test. One veteran counselor who began working at the San Francisco AIDS Health Project in 1986 described the earliest test counseling protocol. During this period, the primary counseling concern was the degree to which positive results could lead to suicidal thoughts. No treatments existed, and scientific understanding of transmission and prognosis of HIV infection was rudimentary.

During the second phase of the CT progam, from 1988 to 1992, the testing program grew very rapidly. As the percentage of positive results declined from double digits to between one and two percent, test counseling was conceived less as a crisis intervention and more in terms of an opportunity for primary prevention. Alternative Test Sites were renamed "Counseling and Testing Sites" to reflect the programs change in 98 focus. During this period, counseling served primarily to disseminate basic information about HIV and AIDS and safer sex guidelines.

Unlike the early years, the role of the counselor was primarily didactic, providing each client with a standard body of information about the test, the availability of new treatments, and ways to reduce their risk. Despite the rising costs of providing individualized counseling, funding remained essentially flat for the period. For example, in California, clinics received the same level of reimbursement from 1985 until 1997. Since clinics were reimbursed according to the number of tests provided, and reimbursements did not keep up with inflation, there was no incentive to improve or even maintain current levels of quality or duration of prevention counseling.

In 1990, the state of California began collecting client demographic information using client profile forms. This marked the beginning of a trend toward bureaucratization of CT services. Because no other primary prevention services existed in most jurisdictions, and testing budgets appeared bottomless, it became a routine practice to encourage clients to test regularly. Over half of all people testing in publicly-funded clinics were low or no-risk clients. Still more people tested regularly at private doctors offices where prevention counseling was generally non-existent.

With each new wave of treatment advances, the rationale for test counseling increasingly shifted toward secondary prevention. Routine testing, it was assumed, would allow for early detection of HIV infection and thus maximize the potential benefits of new treatments. Yet recent research questions the utility of testing for secondary prevention. In a study of positive testers in eight states, Bindman and colleagues found that a large percentage of the HIV infected population delay treatment as well as testing until after AIDS symptoms have developed. The average time between an HIV-positive test and an AIDS diagnosis is 400 - 700 days.

Clearly, the new treatments are no panacea. They have many side effects and frequently fail once the virus develops resistance. The need for strict adherence combined with the side effects and questionable effectiveness makes the decision whether to enter treatment extremely complex. A test result disclosure session is not sufficient in itself to counsel people who test positive to actively seek treatment. Although CT is often advocated as an important gateway into treatment, this recent data suggests that CT is clearly not enough.

As the testing program grew rapidly, renewed attention focused on the content and quality of the counseling and referrals to other services. Two meta-analyses of the effects of testing on behavior change showed little positive effect, particularly for those who tested negative. Wolitski acknowledged that test counseling in the majority of studies was information-based education rather than client-centered counseling. The results of these studies suggested that hundreds of millions of dollars were being spent on an intervention that lacked a recognized standard and appeared to have limited efficacy. The opportunity costs of funding such a large and ineffective prevention policy are enormous.

Most counseling consisted merely of admonishments to use condoms, and the same level of services were provided to low and high risk clients alike. There was little effort to assist people in reducing high risk behavior. Many people with persistent high risk behavior were given condoms and advised to return for repeat testing in 6 months. Several counselors expressed frustration that people with high risk behaviors continued those behaviors but returned for testing every 6 months to see if they had become infected.

The confusion and frustration over the limits of the test counselor's role is not simply due to lack of training. Test counseling was never intended to serve as a stand alone behavioral intervention. Training stresses the importance of referrals to other prevention services that can provide more intensive counseling over multiple sessions. However, according to the CDC external review, "referral services for people with high risk behaviors were usually non-existent. When they did exist, counselors at the CTRPN sites were unaware of them". Thus, testing is encouraged in order to assess the client's need for other prevention services, yet no referrals are made.

Because a continuum of prevention services is lacking, test counseling is increasingly seen as a primary prevention intervention in itself, rather than a gateway to other, more-targeted and effective services. Due to political resistance to publicly funded community-level AIDS education, testing remains the only politically acceptable prevention modality in most jurisdictions. In a political context that favors surveillance and easily quantifiable individual-level interventions, test counseling will naturally be funded over other interventions regardless of what research says about its effectiveness.

As the only HIV prevention intervention in most jurisdictions, test counseling is held to the same outcome standards as science-based, multi-session, behavioral interventions. Such expectations are a set up for failure because test counseling, as practiced in the field, lacks the resources for training and supervision needed for proof of concept studies such as the CDC's Project Respect or HIVNET's Project EXPLORE.

Without adequate funding and leadership to implement a coordinated approach to targeted, community-level HIV prevention that includes expanded access to medical and social services, the over-reliance on testing alone will not slow the epidemic. This was a radical departure from the centralized and competitive disbursement system that was run entirely by the CDC. Although the CDC still oversees the activities of the planning groups and provides guidance and technical support, local planning groups are free to set the levels of funding for testing and other prevention activities.

Under the new local planning system, which began in 1995, allocations for testing and counseling have dropped significantly and more emphasis has been placed on more targeted outreach and evidence-based prevention interventions. California's testing program is no exception. The contradictions of the test counseling program were evident in Truax's justifications for the changes. Despite what his superiors in the state government have believed, Truax recognized the limited role of testing and counseling for changing behavior, yet also recognized that repeat testing is the only referral. And one of the things that has been good for counseling and testing over the years is that we recognize that counseling and testing is not the cureall.

A psychologist by training, Steve Truax is director of prevention research for the State Office of AIDS and oversees the large database of client information collected by counselors. Truax's task is a difficult one. He must balance the state's need for population level surveillance with the needs of the counselor to provide adequate risk reduction counseling. As the designer of the risk assessment form, Truax is in a pivotal position within the grid of power relations that flow back and forth between the CDC and the local health departments that collect the data. He must stress the importance of test counseling to stakeholders who are continually looking to cut expensive and controversial programs, while keeping in mind the needs of test site administrators to provide services and meet their budgets.

Truax operates in an essentially flat budget environment requiring a great deal of creativity to enhance the quality of the existing framework of service delivery. The rate restructuring offers a good example of this creative allocation of funds. Under the new reimbursement plan money is redistributed from low-risk clients to high-risk clients. "Low" and "high" risk are somewhat arbitrarily defined by the risks checked off on the form by the counselors.

Risk factors that are positively correlated with HIV infection in the database are now distinguished by shaded boxes on the form. According to the new reimbursement protocol, all clients receive the same 20 minute pre-test counseling, however low-risk clients are to receive minimal post-test counseling while higher-risk clients receive enhanced counseling and referrals to other services. Low-risk post-test sessions are not reimbursed at all, while high-risk post test sessions are reimbursed both for prevention counseling and for providing referrals to other prevention services. From the local test site administrator's perspective, the new policy translates into more money for forms that show higher risks.

Truax takes it on faith that test sites will complete forms accurately and counselors will allocate more time for higher-risk clients. Truax goes on to emphasize the importance of repeat testing, not as an opportunity for prevention counseling, but as an opportunity to provide referrals to other services. But herein lies the contradiction.

The terms "client-centered" and "counseling" have largely been emptied of their original meaning when applied to the bureaucratic and clinical context of HIV testing services. The concept of "client-centered counseling" is derived from the psychotherapeutic approach developed by Carl Rogers. Rogers' work represented a radical paradigm shift for psychology that had been focused almost exclusively on diagnostic criteria and psychometric testing. In Rogers' humanist model of counseling, each individual is endowed with an organic capacity for growth and change.

The counselor's role is to feed this natural capacity through empathy and unconditional acceptance. The primary technique of client-centered counseling is to actively listen and reflect the client's narrative in a non-directive manner, thereby providing a safe environment for the client's selfexploration. This non-directive reframing of the client's feelings is not a mechanical repetition of the client's last words, as caricatures of this approach often portray.

The counselor's relationship with the client enables her to clarify the client's feelings without imposing external assessments or values. The term "client-centered" counseling has been used extensively in the literature on test counseling. The context in which Rogers developed his methods is very different from test counseling. HIV is a highly stigmatized, deadly, and transmissible infection with unprecedented economic, public health, clinical, and legal consequences both for individuals and society.

This unique context makes a twenty-minute HIV counseling session very different from the types of problems that client-centered counseling was developed to address over multiple, and comparatively lengthy, sessions. The development of a counselor-client relationship is the crucial element of client-centered counseling. In a test counseling situation, however, there are simply too many tasks for the counselor to complete within a small window of time. These tasks have nothing to do with the client's issues but serve the institution's need for consent, charting, billing and data collection.

Building a working relationship on trust and empathy is simply not possible within the institutional framework of a public health service. Test counseling also differs from a therapeutic relationship in that it is provided to clients who have not requested it. It simply comes as part of the package if you request an HIV test. The clients of HIV counsellors may not have brought 'problems' that they wish to talk about and so may often adopt a more 'passive' role.

Rogers' client-centered counseling is antithetical to behavioral approaches typical of public health. The latter approach typically imposes a top-down assessment of the client's needs and capacities for change. In a top-down model, the therapeutic relationship is used to make the client accept the counselor's analysis of the situation. Public health targets individuals for intervention, not to help individuals but in the interests of the larger population. At the core of biopower is a fundamental distrust of the subject, who is in fact no longer a subject but an aggregate of risk factors.

There is, in fact, no longer a relation of immediacy with a subject because there is no longer a subject. What the new preventative policies primarily address is no longer individuals but factors, statistical correlation's of heterogeneous elements. They deconstruct the concrete subject of intervention, and reconstruct a combination of factors liable to produce risk. Their primary aim is not to confront a concrete dangerous situation, but to anticipate all the possible forms of eruption of danger. 'Prevention' in effect promotes suspicion to the dignified scientific rank of a calculus of probabilities.

In public health discourse, individuals are invariably defined in terms of a deficiency - a lack of information, socialization, or self-efficacy. By contrast, Rogers worked from the bottom up, working from within the client's phenomenal world to guide the client's own problem solving capacities. Despite the fundamental incompatibility of the humanist approach of counseling with the behaviorist and population focused approach of public health, "counseling" and "self-help" have increasingly been adopted as techniques of biopower applied at the level of the individual - what we might call "pastoral biopower." Public health services have become increasingly decentralized, privatized, and community based.

With deinstitutionalization, state-sponsored family planning, genetic testing, and the "war on drugs," there has grown a need for individual, face-to-face interventions by street-level bureaucracies. With the rise of individual focused medical and case management services to address a growing list of social and ethical problems-teen pregnancy, drug use, delinquency, and new reproductive screening technologies-counseling techniques were appropriated from the psychotherapeutic context and applied in clinical, judicial, and social work contexts.

Once these new individualized services offered in a clinical context, a new cadre of para-professional "counselors" was created. In the case of substance abuse and AIDS, "counselors" were recruited from target populations, thus emphasizing life experience over clinical or theoretical training in counseling. This emphasis reflected the need to serve a large population using lower paid workers-ideally volunteers- because such programs lacked the funds to hire professionally trained counselors.

Moreover, trained professionals were, for the most part, neither willing nor trained to work with stigmatized and marginalized populations. In essence, counseling in a clinical context is recast from a therapeutic encounter to a highly routinized assessment, screening, and consent process that facilitates the deployment of a clinical intervention, be it abortion, HIV testing, or genetic testing. A number of interesting parallels can be drawn between abortion counseling and test counseling.

As Simmonds and Joffe reveal, counseling in a clinical environment is hampered by its relatively low status compared to the biomedical interventions. Abortion counselors work under time constraints since their work has to follow the dictates of the medical/surgical staff. Abortions counselors are typically not allowed to accompany their clients during the procedure, as if all the emotional issues are expected to be resolved by the time the medical staff is ready to do the procedure.

Simmonds noted how a strong punitive discourse carries over from the medical staff into the work of the counselors. The existence of counselors, ostensibly attending to the emotional and educational needs of the clients, only serves to reinforce the judgmental silence of the medical staff. The counselor's task is to produce a docile subject to facilitate the workflow of the medical staff. Counseling in both contexts is held to unrealistic expectations for changing complex behaviors such as unprotected sex.

Many abortion counselors express frustration and even anger whenever clients seek repeat abortions. Clients are blamed whenever services fail to change sexual behaviors that counselors deem problematic. Despite the best intentions of counselors to be non-judgmental and "client-centered," the top-down, normalizing discourse that sees hormonal birth control as the only solution, renders such efforts meaningless.

The CDC released new guidelines for "client-centered" counseling " beginning in 1992. The new guidelines placed more emphasis on behavioral and counseling theory and explicitly stressed the inadequacy of information-based approaches. The clientcentered model was clearly at odds with current practice and was a welcome change from the perspective of program managers and stakeholders alike. It is difficult to argue with the notion that counselors should regard clients as human beings and tailor the sessions to their particular needs.

Yet, without specific reference to the local practices, many of which make the transition to a client-centered model difficult if not impossible, these new guidelines have limited relevance. The new guidelines attempted to combine several approaches that are incompatible with each other as well as with the institutional culture of test counseling. From the counselors' perspective, the new standards placed an 112 enormous and unprecedented expectation on counselors to be able to change sex- and drug-related risk behavior within the limits of a twenty-minute session.

Despite the incompatibility of this model with the established practice of test counseling, the "client-centered" approach is now codified in training materials as well as state and federal guidelines for HIV test counseling. The CDC guidelines released in May 1994 offer a broad description of the goals, but are silent on the question of method or technique. Client-centered counseling refers to counseling conducted in an interactive manner responsive to individual client needs. This counseling avoids a preconceived set of points to be made by the counselor and encourages the client to do most of the talking.

The focus is on developing prevention goals and strategies with the client rather than simply providing information. An understanding of the unique circumstances of the client is required-behaviors, sexual identity, race/ethnicity, culture, knowledge, and social and economic status. The revised State of California HIV Counseling and Testing Guidelines provide a more descriptive version of the "client-centered" approach. Two necessary conditions for client-centered counseling are:

— Unconditional positive regard refers to the counselor's respect for, not necessarily approval of, the client's feelings and concerns. If a counselor feels very different than a client regarding a significant issue related to HIV risk, it is imperative that the counselor detach from his/her perspective completely in order to communicate effectively with the client.

— Clients often feel that they understand their "issues," and the counselor may even use the client's own words and images to reflect back that understanding to the client. Although the counselor may disagree with the client's understanding, client-centered framing techniques can help the client begin to reframe his/her issues. This reframing can help the client clarify reality-based issues and risk taking in way that the client finds valuable and usable. Helping the client to do his or her own reframing is the primary object of client-centered counseling .

Client-centered principles are altered to reflect the fundamental distrust of the clients' understanding of their own issues and the privileging of the counselor's unilateral access to "reality-based" expertise. The guidelines correctly stress that remaining "client-centered" is not a laissez-faire attitude as Rogers' non-directive approach is often misunderstood to be. As Susan Dietz explained at a recent CDC workshop on perinatal testing Sometimes there is a misunderstanding that a client-centered interaction is a free-form conversation about anything that happens to come up, such as the weather or what happened to the client that day or something totally unrelated. That is not the point of a client-centered interaction.

The counselor does have a responsibility to keep the session directed toward HIV prevention. What is different about client-centered counseling is that it is the client's HIV prevention issues that become the main topic. Sometimes that is difficult to do, and a counselor does have a responsibility to bring that discussion back to HIV prevention, so that there is a specific prevention goal at the end of the session. There must be a prevention goal, no matter how small-some incremental step should be agreed on by the end of that counseling session.

Hence, the only reframing possible is one that sees risk taking as highly problematic from a public health standpoint, rather than attempting to understand the client's phenomenology of risk behavior. This reframing comes with a host of pre-suppositions about the client's values about risk-avoidance. Unless counselors can disengage from the risk elimination stance taken by public health, and become more empathic it will be difficult for them to enter into an honest dialogue with clients about their risk behaviors.

Trainees were thereby furnished with a new vocabulary with which to translate prevention messages into the appropriate vernacular of the indigene. This cross-cultural sensitivity tended to reify stereotypes about each group's particular cultural risks factors. The enhanced risk-assessment training was provided six months later once novice counselors had gained some experience with clients. This two-day training had been developed in 1994, after the CDC published first client-centered recommendations.

Very different from the first training, this training focused on the problem of "relapse" to unsafe sex and the stages of change model. Through role-plays we learned skills such as assessing the context of risk behaviors, prioritizing the intervention, "constructive confrontation," and how to respect one's limits as a counselor. Where the previous "testing" model was a generic and fact-based curriculum, the updated training emphasized an individually tailored approach to the clients' level of knowledge and even their developmental "stage of change".

The counselors' role as health educator was replaced with their "limited" role as risk reduction counselor. As the new "client-centered training pointed out, Information alone does not lead to behavior change: Behavior change is a complex process. Providing information as the sole, or main, intervention is generally not sufficient to lead a person to change behaviors. Another justification for the de-emphasis of education was that levels of HIV knowledge had increased since the early years of test counseling.

In addition, many clients had already been tested and counseled, making much of the information appear redundant. Indeed many of the clients living in highly impacted areas such as the San Francisco Bay Area knew considerably more about HIV/AIDS than the counselors. Despite the trend toward saturation with HIV prevention information from electronic and print media, HIV information has also become more complex and contradictory.

As clients are exposed to more and more HIV information, test counselors and HIV hotlines are increasingly sought to resolve contradictions or explain the relevance of recent studies reported in the media. Clients also tend to discuss AIDS with other lay people more than before. The democratization of AIDS information has meant that already complex and distorted messages become even more inconsistent. Religious groups actively circulate "science" on the lack of efficacy of condoms in order to promote abstinence messages.

Therefore, a crucial task for HIV test counselors is to help clients understand where they stand in this sea of information and to critically interpret the relevance of prevention messages to their situation. Thus, by no means has the client's need for information diminished. In fact, it could be argued that the counselor's role as educator is more important than ever. Rather than providing information, counselors must provide critical thinking skills that will allow clients to judge the merits of contradictory AIDS information.

While a return to the primarily didactic model of test counseling would be undesireable, counselors cannot assist clients in reducing their risk without making sure the client has an accurate understanding of relevant transmission and risk reduction information. One of the more ironic aspects of the State's "client-centered" model of counseling was the revision of the form to accommodate the new approach. The amount of data required to complete the form was increased several fold. The form became double sided, and the questions increased in both number and complexity.

For example, clients are now asked to detail condom use for oral, vaginal, and anal intercourse with each type of partner-Male, Female, Sex Worker, IDU, HIV positive, and Bisexual Males. The number of recreational drugs surveyed doubled on the new form, meaning that counselors spent considerably more time attempting to explain what the form is asking and why the state needs all this information. For Truax, clientcentered counseling is primarily a question of proper risk assessment, which requires a more complex form.

A key component of the new client-centered approach to HIV counseling is the establishment of a risk assessment process. The risk assessment process HIV counselors now follow to determine the client's HIV prevention needs provides a more complete and useful descriptin of risk patterns than ever before. Few special studies match the thoroughness of this data and the resulting State database is large enough to provide reliable findings for even very small groups.

Although, the form is supposed to recede into the background, the forms are very difficult to fill out accurately without directly asking the clients. Higher risk clients, defined as clients for whom a shaded box is checked on the form, net the clinic double the rate of lower risk clients. Local health departments have an interest in accuracy and consistency in completing the form because their ability to enter the data onto the state database to ensure accurate billing depend on the counselors' thoroughness. The stress on accuracy and completeness is naturally passed along to each counselor by their supervisor For example, on the new form counselors are encouraged to probe more about drug use, since certain drugs are flagged as higher risk.

The two-tiered reimbursement system and the complexity of the drug questions make it more likely that counselors will ask these questions, much as if they are completing an epidemiological survey. In terms of counseling strategy, the issue of drug use and its relation to drug use is best addressed in response to the clients' own narratives about their risk behavior. The clients' own narrative, however, is never elicited because the focus is on completing the form using closed-ended "yes" or "no" questions.

Moreover, as drug abuse counselors know, clients are not likely to admit that their drug or alcohol use is "out of control" or even an issue needing to be addressed. By asking clients directly about their drug use, for the purposes of filling out the form, clients are more likely to lie about their drug use. They are also more likely to deny the relevance of their drug use for their risk of unprotected sex. Because counseling occurs one-on-one, with infrequent direct supervision, the form is one of the only ways supervisors can regularly assess a counselor's performance.

Nevertheless, all counselors appeared to use some type of mental checklist as a mnemonic device to structure the session and be sure to provide the client with all the necessary information. Counselors used a set script and clients appeared to sense the rote nature of the interaction and politely allowed the counselor to perform their routines undisturbed. A few counselors took the checklist approach to an extreme, providing each client with a veritable blitz of information, risk reduction advice, and prevention messages that were by and large irrelevant to the client's situation.

For example counselors discussed the risks of neonatal transmission, or the use of certain types of anti-fungal vaginal creams which contain oil-based ingredients even though clients indicated that these were not issues for them or their partners. Counselors using the information blitz format used a number of strategies to justify their approach to the client. A number of counselors asked clients to begin the session by summarizing what they know about how the virus is transmitted. This quiz format is patronizing since it assumes that the client can readily verbalize their knowledge to someone positioned as an expert on the subject.

Clients were generally expected to recite the list of four bodily fluids that can transmit HIV, not merely those with which they might have contact. Most clients avoid the embarrassment of making a mistake and plead ignorance, realizing that the counselor will probably correct them anyway. This allows the counselors to justify their lectures as if the clients had solicited it. Needless to say, those brave clients who do attempt to summarize the modes of transmission are only able to stumble through a sentence or two before the counselor jumps in and proceeds again down the checklist.

This type of checklist pedantry is precisely what the "client-centered" model was intended to displace. Client-centered counseling, as described by the 1997 DHS/OA Guidelines, involves an interactive, highly personalized exchange between client and counselor. Counselors working with clients in a client-centered manner will not be wedded to a preconceived set of points. Rather they will engage in a dialogue that encourages the client to do most of the talking.

If counselors were to actually address these issues in a "client-centered" way, that is by letting the client raise these issues themselves, a test counseling session would probably take several hours, perhaps days. In twenty minutes, the only way to cover a small fraction of these topics is for the counselor to lecture and for the client to remain passive and silent. The proliferation of checklists on the new form reveals the state's ambivalent embrace of client-centered principles and a lack of confidence in their counselors' ability to implement them. The changes to the form also reveal the data fetish that appears to drive the counseling and testing program.

According to the new "client-centered" guidelines, counselors should assist the client in developing a realistic risk-reduction plan. The non-directive, client-centered model is clearly in conflict with the highly directive, behaviorist agenda of risk reduction counseling. As Sikkema and Bissett observe the relevance of various counseling models for HIV test counseling, HIV counseling may include skill development through role-plays, proper use of condoms, or needle hygiene.

These tasks are behavioral or cognitive behavioral by nature. As such, they differ fundamentally from a client-centered approach which does not encourage therapist direction of the client in, for example, behavior rehearsal or homework assignment. The emphasis on behavioral outcomes of test counseling is also reflected on the new 1997 form. In a large way, the form really follows the evolution of counseling.

Like all HIV prevention interventions, effects are difficult to measure. Behavioral interventions typically use some form of pre and post-test instrument to evaluate the short-term impact of an intervention. The difficulty in evaluating the impact of test counseling on behavior has always been the Achilles heel of the CT program. Truax appeared hopeful that new form could provide one way, albeit limited, to assess the outcomes of the test counseling process.

Separating the needs of individual counselors from those of the surveillance program appears to be very difficult from Truax's perspective as an administrator. As his description of the potential uses of behavioral outcomes reveals, the form reflects not only scientific notions of effective methods but also attempts to satisfy the requirements of evaluators and stakeholders for quantifiable outcomes.

Counselors will have completed the risk assessment by the time they discuss the two boxes related to risk reduction plans. This means that the context for the discussion of future plans will be the inventory of the clients' lifetime risks just completed. This is not the ideal context that encourages a sense of self-efficacy. In order to establish realistic risk reduction goals the clients' past successes in reducing their risks should be the context framing the discussion, rather than their past failures. This is clearly reflected in the CDC's prevention counseling training that is meant to update the client-centered model.

Nowhere on the new form is there a space to record the client's successful steps in avoiding risks. Yet it is these successes that must serve as the basis for any discussion about the future risk reduction plan. It is also unclear why so much emphasis is placed on achieving immediate, measurable results. The interval between pre-test and results disclosure produces a great deal of stress for clients.

Counselors see this period as a liminal time when the issues discussed at the pre-test session prompt clients to reflect on their past behaviors. Clients may interpret a negative result as a validation of past strategies rather than a cause for reflection and change. In the near future, this issue will be moot. As soon as rapid testing technologies are licensed and adopted at testing centers, the interval between pre- and post-test counseling will disappear.

The fact that counselors are supposed to grade clients on a behavioral homework assignment reveals the extent to which counselors are held to the same standard as multisession behavioral interventions. As Sikkema and Bisset observe, several significant aspects of HIV counseling offer challenges to a "pure" client-centered approach. First, the short duration and limited frequency of counseling sessions in HIV CT provide a less than optimal opportunity to develop and implement a behavior change plan based on a good therapeutic relationship. Second, the need to disseminate critical risk transmission information requires a directive counseling style.

The expectation that clients will change their behavior immediately would not even be appropriate for an intervention that involves a true counseling relationship. Moreover, clients are unlikely to develop a constructive relationship with a state data-collector within a few minutes. The emphasis on grading contributes to an already patronizing dynamic that is antithetical to the Rogerian notion of "unconditional positive regard."

Counselors devote a large percentage of the session attending to the absurdity of a number of questions on the form. The logic of the form reflects the data software it feeds, and the logic of a population based, epidemiological survey is completely foreign to the clients' "frame" for their "issues."

The temporal logic of the form is also a frequent source of confusion for clients. The form asks about the occurrence of behaviors over the entirety of the client's life. Thus risks that may have occurred years in the past, and even though previous negative tests may have rendered these past risks moot, these past risks must be divulged in great detail and recorded on the current form. Only those risks that have occurred since a few months before the last test are relevant for a focussed counseling discussion.

The temporal logic of the form forces counselors to juggle multiple time frames. This is especially difficult on busy shifts since the current client's history tends to blend together with the previous client. Because most counselors use the form as a risk assessment tool, past risks that may be irrelevant to the clients current concerns or reason for testing can take on an unwarranted significance. As a result, the relevance of the client's current situation in relation to their decision to re-test is glossed over.

The counselor's reliance on the form to assess the client's risk distorts the time perspective of the session. For example, in the following extract the client describes the current context of his test in terms of a) a rumor that his previous girlfriend may not have disclosed certain risks and b) his concern about having unprotected sex with his current partner. Instead of following up on these issues, the discussion is mired in confusion over the relevance of past risks.

The counselor, apparently filling out the form during this exchange, begins to explain the temporal parameters of the form: any risk over his entire life. The client hears this information as a probe about past risks and answers defensively, stressing the word "normal" several times. Clients cannot change past risk behavior but do have control over current risks. The counselor's efforts to revisit the past will invariably cause the client to put up defenses. A valuable opportunity for client-centered counseling is lost whenever the form reframes the session in terms of the form or past risks and ignores the client's current concerns.

"Constructive confrontation" is a technique advocated by the state in their recent "client-centered" counselor training manuals. This technique serves to point out contradictions within the clients' narrative or between their statements and their body language. In form-centered counseling, however, the client is not provided an opportunity to assess their risk in a narrative format and it is left to the form to define the client's reality. As a result clients are confronted with the form's decontextualized assessment of their risk practices, rather than with their own phenomenological experience of a coherent risk averting strategy.

The data collection form makes client-centered counseling difficult because it impedes the counselor's ability to elicit a narrative from the client. Ironically, it is the delicacy of the questions themselves that reinforces the didactic model of test counseling. Counselors feel awkward when asking clients about HIV risks, and this is commonly reflected in the counselors' distancing strategies. This can be seen in the tendency of many counselors to explain the epidemiological justification for the questions. Thus, the interactional problems created by the delicate nature of the questions lead counselors to treat each question as part of a generic checklist.

The client's participation in the session is limited to providing the appropriate answer and passively listening to epidemiological factoids that each question is "getting at." Given the clinical context in which test counseling occurs it should not be surprising that traditional doctor patient communication formats would occur. The client's passivity in the face of the physician's greater technical knowledge and experience in assessing risk fits with the client's expectations of a highly bureaucratic and form driven medical system.

In his analysis of pediatric clinics in the UK and US, Strong notes the importance of forms in structuring clinical interaction between the parent of the patient and the provider. Doctors and nurses worked with thc form openly displayed and ticked off items one by one as they were covered. The presence of the form and of an official pen hovering over it defined the nature of the parental task: the production of brief answers that could be filled in as quickly and efficiently as possible.

The counselor serves as a tool of the form and the surveillance apparatus it serves. It is to the counselor's advantage to keep this dual frame when filling out the form. The counselor can use the form to ask questions that would otherwise seem out of context and inappropriate, and yet the counselor must also maintain rapport with the client. To do this, counselors ally themselves with the client against the form and yet frequently justify the questions by explaining their purpose.

The challenge for the counselors is to use the state warrant when it is useful, and yet be able to distance themselves from the state when it does not serve their strategy, for example when attempting to confront the client in a non-judgmental way. The form requires counselors to maintain two simultaneous roles and this can be a challenge for even the most skilled counselor. This dual frame limits the counselor's ability to be genuine with the client.

Counselors rely on the state form as warrant to ask awkward questions and frequently use the "we recommend" to give their advice more weight. However, when counselors subsequently position themselves as allies with the client against the state or the clinic-for example by not rushing the session along, being "sex positive," or even "client-centered"-the effort rings hollow against the juridical, sex-negative and depersonalized context of the risk assessment.

Guidelines for Psychologists

In developing countries, Psychologists have been a part of the school system. Originally, the mandate of psychologists in the schools was to address the needs of learning-disabled students, estimated to be approximately 5 percent of the total student population. School psychologists are an integral and important part of the student services team, as well as of the district's organizational structure. School psychologists provide a wide variety of both educational and clinical services to districts, school staff, students, and their families.

School psychologists have an understanding and knowledge of educational policies and issues that stem from working within the educational system have an understanding of schools as a result of maintaining regular and direct contact with students, teachers, parents, and the community have long-term contact with chronic situations (i.e. disruptive behaviour disorders, learning disabilities) within the school system and are regularly exposed to how these situations affect the classroom on a day-to-day basis bring a psychological approach to the analysis of students' behaviour problems; that is, a scientific, research-based and measurable approach to the study of human behaviour and learning have the tools to systematically measure change in behaviour over time have the training to carry out psychological assessment of students' cognitive and learning styles for the purpose of educational planning have the training to recognize, diagnose, and intervene with various childhood behaviour and learning disorders consult with others involved with students to make achievable and appropriate recommendations and plans for students support the parents and teachers in the implementation of recommendations and plans maintain liaisons with other agencies in the community to ensure comprehensive service-delivery to students, parents, and teachers with whom they work develop, consult, and participate in programs designed to intervene in crisis and emergency situations in schools - act as a psychological resource to the educational system

School psychologists provide services and interventions to all students in the school system by following a primary prevention, intervention, and postvention service-delivery model. School psychologists enhance the ability of all students to have opportunities for success in school, develop the skills to perform well in school, and receive recognition for their efforts. School psychologists intervene with the whole school population through primary prevention measures such as anti-violence awareness programs, wellness promotion, personal safety and safe-school programs, and family support initiatives.

There are some students in a school who will require more direct intervention. This might take the form of assessment for learning, behavioural, developmental and emotional problems and subsequent program development to address the specific needs identified by the school and through the assessment results. In addition, there may be need for referral to and liaison with community professionals and agencies who might be appropriate to meet the students' medical and counselling needs. There may also be need for parental support.

Some students have need of specialized and immediate assistance. Students at risk of leaving or removal from school (i.e. those with severe disruptive behaviour disorders) have clearly passed the place where the usual interventions can be expected to be helpful. They require what might be termed postvention or services for acute/chronic problems. They need more intensive supports in the form of alternative education programs, on-going counselling services, drop-out recovery and follow-up support, and possible family preservation interventions. While these would not likely be delivered directly by the school psychologist, they would be done in direct consultation with the school psychologist.

School psychologists serve the total population of the school community by drawing on the full content of their training and directing their skills differentially. This breadth of preparation and service-delivery is the key contribution of school psychologists to their clients.

Because they work directly in the educational setting, school psychologists are familiar with the unique characteristics, delivery systems, and current educational policies of the school system. School psychologists work with school, district, and community-based teams, and bring a unique perspective on child development, combined with a research-based system for problem solving.

School psychologists complement the different training and approaches of other team members in providing the most effective and comprehensive service to children and adolescents in the schools. School psychologists support students and teachers in a variety of ways that have an impact on a student's learning and behaviour in the classroom.

Levels of Intervention For School Psychologists

1. *Student-Focused Indirect Intervention*

Focus - To work with parents and teachers in planning educational and behavioural interventions for individual students.

Consultation - School psychologists consult with teachers and administrators in discussing concerns related to individual student or class behaviour and learning difficulties.

Program planning - School psychologists participate in program-planning meetings and case reviews for individual students. Psychologists provide advice on how to adapt the curriculum and make accommodations to meet a student's learning style, cognitive profile, developmental level, or behavioural needs.

Parent contact - School psychologists consult with parents of students with behaviour, socio-emotional, and learning difficulties regarding concerns, intervention strategies, and provision of information to better understand the student.

Goal setting - School psychologists interpret their assessment findings and use them to help to establish realistic goals based on a student's strengths and needs.

Teacher assistance - School psychologists consult with teachers and suggest teaching strategies based on the specific nature of the student's learning or behavioural difficulty.

Interagency networking - School psychologists collaborate and coordinate with other agencies to provide comprehensive services to the child. Referrals - School psychologists facilitate referrals to other agencies and professionals, as needed.

2. *Student-Focused Direct Intervention*

Focus - To work directly with the student either via a psychological assessment and/or in a therapeutic or counselling relationship.

Individual counselling and therapy - School psychologists use techniques such as cognitive behavioural therapy, relaxation therapy, rational emotive therapy, and social skills training that have a research-based efficacy. Individual counselling and therapy also involve psychoeducational techniques designed to help the student and others have a better understanding of the problem.

These may also include counselling focused on personal issues, prevention, and planning for the future.

Group behaviour skills development - School psychologists often meet the needs of a number of students by organizing small groups which focus on social skills training, anger management training, stress management, and the effects of divorce on children, for example. Individual psychological assessment - Individual psychological assessment includes the administration and interpretation of standardized psychological tests (i.e.cognitive development, memory, language, executive functioning, visual perception, auditory perception, language development, visual motor skills, academic attainment, socio-emotional and behaviour adjustment).

Assessment also includes classroom observations, file review, gathering case history information through interviews and checklists, and reviewing other professional assessments of the child. The data from a psychological assessment serve as the basis for recommendations concerning intervention strategies for parents and teachers.

3. School-Wide Intervention

Focus - To work with a school toward improving the delivery of services in meeting students' mental health and learning needs.

Liaison - The school psychologist acts as a liaison with, and/or serves on school-based student services teams.

Collaboration - The school psychologist collaborates with teachers and administrators to support inclusion of exceptional students within the school.

In-service education - The school psychologist provides school-based in-service training to teachers and administrators in such areas as behaviour management strategies, collateral assessment methods, understanding exceptionalities, and stress management.

Prevention - The school psychologist advises on school-wide prevention and intervention programs that facilitate the development of a positive school environment.

Consultation - The school psychologist consults with teachers and administrators in the provision of information about learning styles and behaviours commonly associated with various identified learning, socio-emotional, and behavioural problems.

Best practices - The school psychologist provides information related to current research on interventions in the area of children's mental health and various exceptionalities.

Planning - The school psychologist participates in planning and implementing school-wide screening and assessment programs. Postvention - The school psychologist coordinates debriefing and defusing of students and staff following a tragic event which affects the school as a whole. Teaching - The school psychologist facilitates parenting programs.

4. District/System-Wide Intervention

Focus - To improve the system as a whole in its effectiveness in dealing with students' mental health and learning difficulties.

In-service education - The school psychologist provides district-wide in-service training for educational staff on child development, behaviour management, exceptionalities, and assessment.

Screening - The school psychologist develops and carries out early screening programs in the schools.

Evaluation - The school psychologist assists with data collection and evaluation of system-wide mental health and special education interventions.

Best practices - The school psychologist reviews current educational and psychological research on topics of relevance to educators.

Intervention programs - The school psychologist assists in developing, implementing, or consulting with system-wide intervention programs (i.e. conflict resolution, social skills, bullying programs, drop-out prevention, violence prevention, crisis intervention, alternative education programs). Outreach - The school psychologist develops and implements parenting programs.

Networking - The school psychologist serves on multiagency committees and programs, and collaborates with various agencies in program planning. Advocacy - The school psychologist advocates for children with learning, socio-emotional and behavioural exceptionalities.

5. Research

The training of a psychologist stresses the use of a scientific research-based approach to the study of human behaviour. As a result, psychologists are in a position to serve in both an advisory capacity or to have direct responsibility for carrying out research projects in the educational setting. More specifically, psychologists can advise on or carry out planning, data collection, data analysis, interpretation of results, and translation of findings into practical applications.

Psychologists have training in statistical analysis and techniques, and social sciences research design. They are, therefore, in a unique position within the educational setting to design and implement research projects for a variety of purposes. In particular, psychologists can evaluate the effectiveness of various types of behavioural and educational interventions, as well as the effectiveness and validity of various group and individual assessment tools. A psychological assessment is an objective measure of samples of behaviour. It may include the evaluation of

— social adjustment

— emotional status

— personality

— cognitive functioning

— language processing

— information processing

— visual-motor development

— executive functioning (attention, impulse control)

— aptitude

— academic achievement

— motivation

Information obtained in an assessment is used to plan specific instructional and behavioural interventions for the student, as well as to set realistic, attainable goals. The psychological assessment, along with information from numerous sources and other professionals, contributes to a further understanding of the whole child. A psychological assessment involves the use of formal, psychodiagnostic procedures requiring a considerable degree of training, expertise, and continual upgrading of knowledge.

Psychological tests and procedures utilized in an assessment are scientific and research-based tools. In the hands of inexperienced, unsupervised, or unqualified individuals, there is potential for serious consequences such as misdiagnosis and improper interpretation of assessment data. This could lead to either ineffective interventions or possibly harmful interventions.

There are a number of excellent academic tests that can be comfortably and competently administered by resource teachers and guidance counsellors. Results of these tests offer teachers valuable direction for immediate interventions with students, as well as providing substantial collateral information for a psychological assessment. School psychologists, with their specialized training in psychometrics, can be helpful on a consultative basis, assisting resource teachers and guidance counsellors in interpreting scores on various standardized academic tests.

The provision of in-service training in the areas of statistics, test construction, validity, reliability, and the meaning of various scores (e.g. standardized scores, percentile ranks, grade equivalency) is another service that can be provided by school psychologists. A service-delivery model that requires an initial consultation with the school psychologist prior to an assessment referral is recommended. This process allows for a more timely response, as several consultations can occur in the time it takes to do one assessment.

This process also allows the psychologist to have input into establishing the need for, and the goals of, the assessment, as well as assisting the school in determining assessment priorities. In other cases, a review of the student's file, assistance with interpretation of school-based educational assessments, and consultation may be adequate to address the concerns. In all cases, a consultation allows for some immediate intervention to take place, even if the student has to be placed on a waiting list for an assessment.

School psychology is an educationally based support service. Requests for school psychological services, including assessments, should go through school teams. The school team is in the best position to establish school referral priorities and the team should screen all requests for formal assessment. School psychologists do not accept direct referrals for assessment from parents or professionals outside of the school system, although preliminary consultation is welcome.

Situations that might warrant a referral to a school psychologist include the following:

1. The classroom and resource teachers have worked with the student and have carried out some individual educational assessments. The student is not responding to the strategies outlined in the special education plan and teachers do not know why. School personnel believe that they require more information regarding the student's learning style, and cognitive and developmental profile in order to enhance the student's special education program.

2. Teachers are uncertain about the student's developmental level and need assistance in developing realistic long-term expectations for the student.

3. Teachers suspect that the student may have a neurologically based disorder (e.g. Autism, Attention Deficit Hyperactivity Disorder, Tourette's Syndrome, Mood Disorder) that is having a significant impact on the student's adjustment. Diagnostic confirmation, advice on needed referrals to other professionals, and intervention strategies are required.

4. There is a conflict between the teachers' and the parents' expectations and perceptions of a student's learning and/or behavioural needs. In some of these cases, a psychological evaluation is believed to be required to provide objective and standardized information to further clarify the student's needs and to assist in resolving the conflict.

5. Teachers believe that the parents are having difficulty understanding or accepting their child's needs. Involving a school psychologist in such discussions can assist the parents to develop a better understanding of their child's strengths and needs and the value that special programming can provide.

6. A student has serious behavioural and/or emotional problems, and the teachers want to know what (neurological, socio-emotional, environmental, and personality) factors might be affecting the student's behaviour. An assessment in this case may lead to referral to other specialties, suggestions of specific types of intervention strategies, or identification of the most appropriate therapeutic or counselling interventions.

District personnel determine the services they require from the psychologists serving their schools regardless of where the psychologists are employed. The types of services provided by a school psychologist will depend on a number of factors, including the training, experience, and the interests of the psychologist, as well as the priorities established by the school district(s) and schools served by the psychologist.

Student-Focused Consultation

Access to school psychological services for consultation, assessment, or other service normally follows a referral process. Teachers are usually the first observers of learning, social-emotional, or behavioural difficulties in the school setting. When a teacher has a concern about a student, a referral form is completed which outlines areas of concern and interventions attempted to address the need.

School-based team meetings, which usually involve an administrator, resource teacher, guidance counsellor, classroom teacher(s), and perhaps a district student services representative, afford an opportunity to address these concerns. As a result of this collaborative process, a formal referral for school psychological services may be initiated. Psychologists may be available for informal consultation and classroom observation throughout this process. Referrals for service from school psychologists are usually forwarded to the school district office.

Since psychological services in schools may be provided by either district-based psychologists or by psychologists from the Department of Family and Community Services, two referral processes exist. Each district has its own referral form used to access district-based psychological services. A standard provincial referral process, however, is used to access Department of Family and Community Services psychologists. This referral form is usually completed by a classroom teacher, signed by the school principal, and forwarded to a designated school district liaison person.

Access to school psychological services in response to system-wide or school-wide concerns is usually initiated by school and/or district administrators. In districts where there is a supervising psychologist, services are normally coordinated by this individual, who works closely with other district supervisors. Another forum for the access of school psychological services is through a collaborative process involving other members of the district student services team.

Psychologists follow a broad science-practitioner education in the areas of foundations of learning, behaviour and individual differences, research methodology, and program evaluation. School psychologists are unique in having training and experience that facilitates an understanding of both mental health and educational issues. They provide an integrated service that addresses the whole child.

Mental health issues not only have a major impact on a child's behaviour in school but also can seriously impact learning. In turn, learning difficulties impact on a student's social, emotional, and behavioural adjustment. In both instances, written and oral examinations must be successfully completed before an individual becomes licensed as a psychologist. Individuals who are eligible for licensing and are being supervised by a psychologist during their internship are referred to as "Residents in Psychology."

A psychological assessment involves much more than mere administration and scoring of tests. Observations of important aspects of test behaviour such as anxiety, fatigue, attentional and motivational factors are very important. The psychologist must be sensitive to the effects of the assessment procedures on the student. Special techniques are often required to elicit optimal performance from some children.

The interpretation of the student's performance has to take into consideration a variety of factors that influence performance and integrate these factors into a larger context of knowledge concerning test construction, theoretical knowledge of child development, learning theory, psychological processes and child exceptionality. An experienced and well-trained psychologist can do this best.

A thorough understanding of statistics and psychometrics (test construction) is required to interpret psychological tests accurately. In order to interpret various types of scores, it is necessary to have an understanding of how they are derived, what they mean and how they compare to other types of statistical measures. In addition, the examiner must be capable of reviewing the technical merits of selected instruments in terms of such characteristics as validity, reliability, standardization and test construction.

As new instruments come on the market, this particular capability becomes even more essential. It is incumbent on psychologists to be able to demonstrate that the tests and procedures used to arrive at diagnosis and interpretation are valid. Appropriate interpretation of psychological assessments requires familiarity with new developments and with current independent studies of assessment instruments.

Accurately making psychological diagnosis is a very challenging task, even for an experienced clinician. The diagnosis of many disorders may result in some very specific prescriptions for therapy, prognosis for outcome and medication treatment. Non-psychologists, including teachers, should be very careful about making suggestions that a child may have some specific type of psychological disorder. The Diagnostic and Statistical Manual of Mental Disorders (DSM IV) recognizes over 40 psychiatric disorders usually first diagnosed in childhood. In addition, there are also a number of psychological disorders that may be diagnosed in both adults and children.

Those engaged in psychological assessments must take into consideration ethical standards, confidentiality and protection of the student's rights. Informed consent from a student of legal age or from a parent or legal guardian of a younger student is absolutely essential. Information obtained from assessments should only be shared with those persons involved with the teaching and learning process of the student. Psychological reports are the property of the school district, and should be kept in secure areas. Once a student is no longer in school, there must be clear policies regarding the length of time a psychological report and/or file is kept.

Individuals, including psychologists, administering psychological assessments may find themselves required to defend or explain their assessment in a court of law. School personnel will find that they are on much safer ground if the individuals that they employ to carry out or to supervise psychological assessments are qualified to do so. No court will challenge the right of a licensed psychologist to carry out the accepted tasks of his/her profession. However, individuals performing tasks of a psychological nature who are not licensed or qualified to do so, may find themselves in a very vulnerable position.

A specific responsibility of school psychologists involves the ethical requirement to protect test security and to ensure that access to psychological tests is restricted to licensed psychologists or residents in psychology. All distributors of psychological tests have restrictions on the purchase of different types of instruments. School districts employing psychologists must take reasonable steps to ensure that the purchase and distribution of psychological tests are for the use of psychologists or residents in psychology only.

It is the logical and statutory right of every doctor in training to be offered career counselling - using the term in its broadest sense. But it is obviously logical in any comprehensive training system that careers counselling should be offered as an integral part. This is especially so in medical training which starts young, lasts for many years; is expensive; and as the training progresses, more and more career options present themselves.

In recent years medical training has become much more structured with the advent of the Calman system for speciality training and the clarification of training in general practice, with both systems involving a good deal of monitoring and mentoring. In reality, there are still baffling variations within training and it is difficult for juniors to obtain a comprehensive picture in order to assist them in choices. Providing such a comprehensive picture is one of the more obvious functions of careers counselling. However, it has a number of other functions to fulfil: -

— As a purely functional aspect of informing the recipient. This provides a framework on which to make contact and should leave the recipient feeling that something useful has been obtained.

- As a means of contact between senior and junior staff. Current philosophy is that this should be an ongoing process but the reality is that changes in the work patterns of seniors increasingly reduces the opportunity for contact and deliberate efforts must be made to build this in, in the form of on-the-job teaching, appraisal and assessment, and careers counselling.
- To provide a route whereby more subtle or personal problems facing the trainee may be brought into discussion. Any such process must be entered into with an element of prior planning so that the senior will have: -
  - Information about the juniors' experience and performance to date. oPreferably some indication from the junior as to what type of specific information will be sought, so that as much as possible can be assembled beforehand.
  - Time: the process takes time and this must be mutually allocated beforehand.

The term careers counselling has been used to embrace a number of different aspects of a process but it is clear that it encompasses several components: -

- Careers information.
- Careers guidance and matters relating to personal development plans. Appraisal and Assessment.
- Counselling - stress and pastoral.

The word "counselling" is used in a variety of settings. Careers counselling it is composed of 4 main pillars: -

Careers Information

This part of the process is based mainly on making available up-to-date and accurate factual information about career structures and opportunities. The type of information that the trainee might reasonably seek in this part of the process is: -

— An account of the existing careers' structure in the career path of speciality chosen and this might be the overall national picture or the local training structures in the Deanery concerned.

— Some estimate of the prospects within that particular training structure.

— Current views of prospects for senior posts.

— The possibilities relating to flexible training.

— Details of study leave policy.

The Clinical Tutor therefore can be very useful in brokering these contacts. In some cases the trainee may simply be asking for factual information and the Clinical Tutor ought to separate in his own mind the presentation of facts and probabilities, as opposed to his own view of what the trainee should do. In any case many trainees will chose their own counsellor when seeking an opinion as to what they should do in a careers context. This is often someone within the chosen speciality with whom they have made good relationships such as a mentor or a senior who has provided a good role model.

The process of seeking and receiving career facts, however, often overlaps into a request for the opinion of the counsellor. Obviously this has to take into account an assessment of the abilities as well as the aspirations of the trainee and is the embodiment of the 2 way nature of the appraisal process. The appraisal process also includes formulation and discussion of career plans and their fulfilment, and this may often widen out into a career counselling process.

It is clear that the Clinical Tutor will not be carrying out all the appraisals and careers counselling for the staff relating to his own Centre, although he should have, and practice, the required skills. His principal responsibility is to ensure that there is a structure in place such that every trainee is actively participating in an appraisal process. This is no mean task and requires a good deal of tact and diplomacy lest Departments feel that their sovereignty is being invaded. Nevertheless, the regulations are quite clearly laid out.

In most Calman structures yearly appraisals for SpRs are the responsibility of the Speciality Training Committees, and undertaken by Educational Supervisors. All other trainees should be appraised regularly by their Educational Supervisors, whether or not appraisal is an integral part of their college curriculum.

Stress Counselling

Personal stresses and strains involved in the medical training have, in the past the often been overlooked by seniors, but in good working relationships juniors should feel that they can discuss a wider range of problems e.g. personal, financial, etc. with a senior in their own profession. Such problems frequently have implications for the career of the individual. Again these may often be taken to a mentor or member of senior staff chosen by the trainee concerned but it is a fact of Clinical Tutors' lives that very often the most difficult problems in this respect will be referred by others to the Clinical Tutor. It is often with these cases that he/she will have to exercise the full extent of his/her own counselling skills and his/her knowledge of the system.

The process may cast the Clinical Tutor in a variety of roles. Generally speaking he will be acting in the role of advocate and mentor, and may be able to use influence to help resolve problems such as inter-personal relationships; at other times he/she may be acting as arbitrator in disputes or arranging for referral for medical or, exceptionally, psychiatric advice. In the latter situations, great care must be taken to observe the ethics and etiquette involved e.g. trainees agreement; involvement of registered GP (if any, v.i.) and appropriate confidentiality.

The difficulties facing overseas doctors, especially those newly-arrived, in the UK are not infrequently overlooked and some attention ought to be paid in Induction Programmes to welcoming such junior doctors and easing their position into a new system and often a different culture. Special attention should be paid to trainees who are constantly claiming sick leave and those who are repeatedly failing examinations. When counselling doctors in training it is appropriate to consider with them how they see their careers fitting in with that of their partners, their plans for starting families or how they manage their careers and their families simultaneously.

These issues are often a source of stress and they should be strongly encouraged to find the solutions in discussion with their partners. It is generally acknowledged that women doctors experience more stress for a variety of reasons including social isolation, gender prejudice, conflict with partner's career, trying to be a "superwoman", the biological clock, the lack of a role model and low self-esteem. These stress factors may lead to under-achievement and where the Clinical Tutor is male, it may be appropriate to seek the aid of a senior female colleague experienced in counselling.

Stress counselling is basically about exploring with a trainee the nature of the problem and helping him/her to understanding the problem so that it can either be resolved, circumvented or accepted. Stress management involves an individual: -

- — Recognising and acknowledging that he/she is experiencing stress.
- — Deciding whether an issue is worth the stress.
- — Taking a long-term view of a problem.
- — Identifying their positive and negative coping mechanisms.
- — Taking up relaxation activities.
- — Organising his/her time efficiently.
- — Identifying who constitutes his/her support system.

The Clinical Tutor may be the person to conduct this, but where this is not the case, he/she should be a supportive facilitator in ensuring that the process is enacted. Formal referral for counselling may be considered. Where an individual feels that he or she is in an inappropriate post or speciality and/or is considering a fundamental career change, consideration can be given to a formal careers counselling process.

In short, careers counselling is very time consuming and you need to have protected time set aside for it. You will find it frustrating some of the time, gratifying at other times, but more importantly your juniors will appreciate it - you know they have a right to it!

1. *Authority*: You are empowered by your contract with the Dean, your job description and the educational contract. There is no reason to feel insecure about initiating and organising career counselling for junior doctors.

2. *Resistance*: You may be confronted by the negativity and lack of co-operation from colleagues who are supposed to help you. There will be a variety of excuses but bear in mind that your colleagues may feel inadequate to the task or feel that you are threatening his/her territorial rights!

3. *Ownership*: Get like-minded colleagues to support you and make sure they are on your Education Committee. College or Speciality Tutors should be actively assisting you in Career Counselling and post Clinical Tutors are useful allies too.

4. *Implementation*: Do it your way to best suit you and your juniors. Your Centre Manager will play a key-role in helping you with the implementation and organisation. Even if you inherit an existing counselling system, do not be afraid to improve or alter it should you wish to do so.

5. *Confidentiality*: The importance of confidentiality cannot be over emphasised. The level of confidentiality can vary according to the circumstances. Clearly there is nothing confidential in spelling out the experience required to sit an examination and this sort of career information might usefully be discussed with a group of trainees. The records of appraisal and assessment should be

confidential, shared and agreed with a trainee who should also have access to the records. However, in future, Deans and Colleges may need to see the records.

6. *Women Doctors*: You may like to suggest to your female consultant colleagues that it might be beneficial for the female juniors that they meet as a group socially so that the consultants can be identified as people that the juniors may seek careers advice from.

7. *Overseas Doctors*: It is easy to overlook the needs of overseas doctors. They may have special needs in being welcomed into the system and there is a danger to assume that they know how it all works.

Bibliography

Beaulieu, L., "Rural Schools and the Workforce Investment Act", *ERIC Clearinghouse on Rural Education and Small Schools,* 2000.

Borch, S., "ISO 9000 in vocational guidance", (in) Bartholomeus, Y. et al. (eds), The Quest for Quality - Towards Joint European Quality Norms, LDC, Leuwaarden, 1995.

CCDF, "Second International Symposium on Career Development and Public Policy", Canadian Career Development Foundation, Ottawa, 2001.

Ford, G., "The Connexions Strategy and All-Age Guidance, Centre for Guidance Studies", University of Derby, 2000.

____________, "Guidance for Adults: Harnessing Partnership Potential", *NICEC Briefing,* Careers Research and Advisory Centre, Cambridge, 2001.

Fretwell, D.H. & Plant, P, "Career Development Policy Models: Synthesis Paper, Second International Symposium on Career Development and Public Policy", *Canadian Career Development Foundation,* Ottawa, 2001

IAEVG, "Ethical Standards, International Association of Educational and Vocational Guidance", Dublin, 1995.

Killeen, J., White, M. & Watts, A.G., "The Economic Value of Careers Guidance", *Policy Studies Institute,* London, 1992.

Kellett, R., & Conger, S., "A Three-Tiered Model of Career Counseling Services, Greensboro", NC, ERIC Clearinghouse on Counseling and Student Services, Greensboro, NC, and

Canadian Career Development Foundation, Ottawa, 1995.

Law, B., "New DOTS - Career Learning Theory for the Contemporary World", NICEC, Cambridge, 2000.

Spracklen, C., Quality and careers guidance in the UK, (in) Bartholomeus, Y. et al. (eds), The Quest for Quality - Towards Joint European Quality Norms LDC, Leuwaarden, 1995.

Watt, G., "Supporting Employability: Guides to Good Practice in Employment Counselling and Guidance, Office for Official Publications of the European Commission, Luxembourg, 1998.

Watts, A.G., "Career guidance and social exclusion: a cautionary tale, British Journal of Guidance and Counselling, Vol. 29, No. 2, 2001.

Watts, A.G., Stern, E. & Deen, N., "Careers Guidance towards the 21st Century: Report of an Anglo-Dutch Consultation within a European Context", CRAC, Cambridge, 1993.

Watts, A., "Guidance trends in Europe", Newscheck, Vol.5 No.2, pp.3-4, 1995.

Index